ONE
BOOK

for

LIFE
SUCCESS

ONE
BOOK

for

LIFE
SUCCESS

Transform yourself into a peak level

VENU G. SOMINENI

Outskirts Press, Inc.
Denver, Colorado

One Book for Life Success
Transform yourself into a peak level

Outskirts Press, Inc.
http://www.outskirtspress.com

ISBN: 978-1-4327-5164-7

Outskirts Press and the "OP" logo are trademarks belonging to Outskirts Press, Inc.

TABLE OF CONTENTS

INTRODUCTION

You know, there is a reason why only 5 percent of the world population is successful and a very small percentage of the population love what they do today. Life is all about a series of choices and experiences. Many people who achieved fortunes in the world are not born rich. Over 70% of the world's billionaires are self-made. According to Forbes magazine (Oct'09), there are 274 billionaires out of the top 400 richest people in America, and they are all self-made. They literally started from zero and made their fortunes from there. If you look at the world population ratio between the rich and the poor-moderate classes, it has always been 5%:95% for centuries. There are thousands of books written in the areas of personal development, success, career growth, inspiration, finance management, investment techniques and more. However, there is no significant change has happened yet and a very few could turn their dreams into reality. There is an absolute gap between the goal setting process and making them into a reality today.

Unfortunately, nobody has born with a manual with a set of best practices and instructions to be successful. A lot of people know the best practices, but unfortunately, very few follow them sincerely. Like the math, there is a true formula for success. I have brought in deep insights, advice on the best habits, practices, and secrets behind successful people and much more in this book.

Knowing the best practices is one thing, but following them sincerely is what makes the real difference. I also added some real life situations and examples which I came across during the course of a decade. At the same time, I tried my best to make this book as simple as possible to avoid any ambiguity to the readers. In reality, nobody would remember the entire content of any book including the author. The take away of every book would just be the summary of it. Unlike the traditional books with over 350 pages, I tried to edit the content very precisely to help you to remember the secrets, best practices, situations and inspiring quotes and more. Throughout this book, I am going to talk about the best practices, habit, tips and quotes to unlock your maximum potential in your day-2-day life.

At the end of the book, your eyes will hopefully be open, and maybe you will realize a lot of things, including: the best practices to be successful; secrets behind successful people; what it takes to be successful; your strengths; your passions; your dreams; where you're stuck now; where you're heading; how to manifest your dreams in a short span of time; what is life all about and much, much more.

I got wonderful feedback from the people who read this book before. I hope you will enjoy the same way, they did. If you like this book, I would request you to spread the word around. Knowledge sharing is the greatest gift you would ever offer to your friends, family, and loved ones. Let's get it started. Happy reading!

Sincerely,
Venu G. Somineni, Author

This book is dedicated to my family, friends, and those who inspired me to bring an author out of me. I love you all.
-Venu G. Somineni, Author

THE HUMAN MIND

Every human being is a sum total of heredity of birth and internal/external influences. There is no way we can change how we're born, but we can change the environment and influences with a strong commitment towards attaining a better life with powerful goals and thoughts.

Every moment the human body is controlled and directed by thought; that is, by orders sent from the brain, where the mind governs the consciousness. The mind is divided into two parts; One being called the conscious part (which directs our bodily activities while we are awake); and the other part being called subconscious part, which controls our bodily activities and thoughts while we are asleep.

Several years ago, the National Science Foundation put out some very interesting statistics about number of thoughts pass through human mind in a day - Human mind produces as many as 12,000 to 50,000+ thoughts per day depending on how 'deep' a thinker you are. Many researchers conclude that, about 90% of these thoughts are very random, useless, and negative. For over 23 years, the Princeton Engineering Anomalies Research Program (PEAR) compiled the evidence that the human mind influences anything it focuses on. It is even more pronounced when bonded teams work together, focusing on a common theme.

Unarguably, the world's fastest supercomputer - the human brain. According to recent study, even the most effective people use only less than 10% of their brain potential. Many scientists are still struggling to create a supercomputer which can mimic as human brain. The brain has over 100 million MIPS worth of processing power while recent super-computers only have a few million MIPS. The average brain can hold over 100 million megabytes of memory. You can plant any number of seeds in your brain. Once you plant, it is your responsibility to groom them well by feeding with positive thoughts.

The entire universe is being created in the form of attraction. People of similar interests, intellect levels and thought processes tend to attract each other in a very little time. We tend to like others, as soon as we shake their hands and even after short conversations. Sometimes, it is hard to digest the short presence of others. It is all about the mind tendencies and harmonious matches. Our brains become magnetized with the dominating thoughts which we hold in our minds, and, by means with which no person is familiar, these "magnets" attract to us the forces, the people, the circumstances of life which harmonize with the nature of our dominating thoughts. Universe does not discriminate between constructive or destructive thoughts. Universe responds according to the input from the subconscious mind.

The bottom line: Write down one recent situation that worked out well and one that didn't. If you answer yourself honestly, you would understand the difference between positive and negative thoughts. Make a habit of reviewing results of every situation in this way and the chances are that you will begin to understand the power of a thought.

GOAL

Firstly, you must form a correct conception of how you want to transform yourself into a peak level. You must cultivate a clear-cut idea of what you want to become. This will give you a definite and clear-cut aim or goal in life. Without such an aim or a specific goal, your life cannot move forward powerfully and progressively. Clarity is what matters. You will be pulled in different directions and your mind will be distracted and a lot of energy will be wasted. Not having a specific goal is like constructing a house without a blueprint. You can avoid all of these if you have a well-defined aim or a set of a few definite objectives. You know what you wish to attain and in which direction to proceed. Therefore, you also understand what is right and what is wrong, what is desirable and what is undesirable, what is to be accepted and what is to be rejected in moving towards your aim in life. Such definiteness gives you great inner strength. It develops will-power. It gives you a positive personality. There will be no more negative trends in your life.

Just remember this simple formula to achieve your goals:

- ❖ Step 1 : Write down your immediate and future goals
- ❖ Step 2 : Prioritize them as per your wish
- ❖ Step 3 : Start working on one goal at a time
- ❖ Step 4 : Focus on priority one first

- ❖ Step 5 : Make a detailed plan and corrective actions and deadline to achieve your immediate goal
- ❖ Step 6 : Share your goal and deadline with your families, friends, loved ones
- ❖ Step 7 : Put all your energies towards achieving this goal
- ❖ Step 8 : Review the progress of your goal every day
- ❖ Step 9 : Believe as if you've already achieved this goal
- ❖ Step 10 : Once you achieve it, celebrate with your loved ones and announce the them the next goal
- ❖ Step 11: Start from Step 1 again

The bottom line: A person without having a goal as deadly as walking in the Amazon forest without a compass.

IMAGINATION

Imagination or visualization is the picturing power of your mind. Your subconscious responds to self-made images/pictures and movies on your mental silver screen. The subconscious mind builds your life. Your imagination is the blueprint and your subconscious mind is the architect.

You are constantly running mental images in your thought process. These images determine your behavior and the kind of life you lead. You have the power to create a new life for yourself in your own imagination. Whatever you can visualize as a movie consciously, you can manifest. Whatever you are picturing in your mind today is what you will be experiencing in the future.

Just think of how the great movies have been made on the silver screens. More than a movie making process - it is also a dream work of story/screenplay writers; imaginative art work; director's creativity; collective dreams of the most talented people and of course the producer's trust on the future project. All these people would be watching the same movie in their imaginations hundreds of times before they bring it into the real screen. You create your own movie for every dream and keep watching it as many times as you possibly can every day. It will be soon manifesting with no doubt.

During the opening of Euro-Disneyland in France in 1992, a reporter asked Walt Disney's grandson, "It is a pity your grandfather is not here to see this opening." His grandson replied, "No, sir. You are wrong. My grandpa had seen this opening before in his imagination multiple times – that is the reason why we are here today."

The bottom line: A person's imagination is only the way to connect with supreme power or Universe. Limitations live only in our minds. In reality, there are no boundaries for imagination.

INNOVATION

Whatever wonders we see in the world today are just the results of the imagination and innovation developed by a single person or group of masterminds. Every innovation creates a lot of opportunities, jobs, lead to even more innovation, and make the world a better place. Creativity rules and controls the world. There are 3 ways to create innovation.

- ❖ Come up with an unique idea (never ever before)
- ❖ Create extensions to the rapid growing businesses with little differentiation factors / value proposition
- ❖ Being in similar kinds of business ventures

Evidently, those businesses which are built based on unique innovation become very famous and rule the roost in their own territory or market within a short span of time. The second and third approaches deal with competition and suffer from true innovation. Innovation always wins over the competition.

The reason behind the unhealthy competition in the corporate world today - just the lack of innovation and no big differentiation factors. If thousands of businesses sell similar kinds of goods or services, it leaves no choice other than fighting with each other. We are all intellectuals within ourselves. If you can put a great effort to bring out the innovation by thinking differently from the rest of the crowd, we can create a world of all innovations and everyone wins.

Innovation is everything. It creates tremendous wealth, job opportunities, and leads to even greater innovations. Look at the things you use daily – electricity, TV, telephone, cell phone, motor bike, car, camera, computers, internet, laptops, ATM, credit cards and millions more – Someone came up innovative idea, and we are enjoying the fruits today. For instance, we cannot imagine a world without a telephone communication today. If Thomas Edison had not invented the light, we might still be reading by gas or candlelight. There are lots of innovations happening across the world now. Ask yourself a simple question – What is your contribution towards current and future generations?

The bottom line: Whatever the industry you passionate about, try to learn deep insights about that industry, products and related services and challenge yourself to come up with a unique idea. Always look for market gaps and current challenges to create a significant change in the world. Every innovation starts with 'What?' not 'how?'. When you remember the importance of an innovation, you can forget about the competition. The existence is always imperfect and innovation is a continuous process; Innovation leads you to reach new peaks, new dimensions, open new doors, and new possibilities.

DREAM

Every burning desire leads to a dream. Dream is the starting point to construct your own world. Once you identify your passion towards creating a unique product/service, then you can start dreaming big in similar lines of your interest. No creation ever came to be without dreams. Ask any successful people you know if they could ever achieve anything without having dreams. Always dream big in whatever you do or have the passion towards.

In simple words, dreaming is all about creating a picture/video/movie with your own imagination and watching it multiple times in your mind every single day. The important aspect of the dream is: It has to be very specific with what you want to achieve. You are the inventor. You are the architect. You are the creator of your own dreams and your imagination is the blueprint of your dreams.

Some people think about too many things at one time. For instance, you may want to buy a big house, acquire millions of dollars worth of cars, and build a big business, and so on. Being a human being, it is your birth right to have desires to earn the best items available in the world. However, you have to focus on one thing at a time. Once you achieve big dreams, the rest will follow automatically.

Socrates was a Classical Greek philosopher. He credited as one of the founders of Western philosophy, he is an enigmatic figure known only through the classical accounts of his students. One of the famous quotes from Socrates, "True knowledge exists in knowing that you know nothing."

Once, a young man asked Socrates the secret of Success. Socrates told the young man to meet him near the river the next morning. They met. Socrates asked the young man to walk with him towards the river. When the water got up to their neck, Socrates took the young man by surprise and ducked him into the water. The man struggled to get out but Socrates was strong and kept him there until he started turning blue. The young man struggled hard and finally managed to get out and the first thing he did was to gasp and take deep breath. Socrates asked "What you wanted the most when you were there?" The young man replied "I wanted to breathe...Air...I wanted air of course."

Socrates said "that's the most secret to success. When you have a desire as badly as you wanted air, you will succeed."

The bottom line: List all your material desires and dreams into two columns separately on a piece of paper. Start associating your material desires into a specific dream. For instance, if you dream yourself doubling your income or creating something unique or identify the ways to make extra money. Have a clear mind set about those in your mind.

DETERMINATION

Mental efficiency depends upon the art of determination. By the power of determination, you can unleash the power of mind to accomplish that what you desire, and you can guard all doors through which failure may enter. All the successful people are very focused on what they do. Most of the people are suffocated by distractions and are unable to find the pearls of success.

If you ever commit yourself to achieve something, make a promise to yourself or your wife or your family or friends or loved ones. It is very hard to achieve anything in this world without being really focused and committed. It takes a lot of effort to build something big, but it takes only few seconds to ruin any effort.

There were many heroes in the corporate world lost their fortune within no time by being distracted by other things. You need to prioritize your actions and focus on those things every single moment. Remember, the world is very competitive. Once your competitor knows you are off the track a bit, you lose the game big time.

The bottom line: Whatever you do, commit yourself to complete it by a specific date and time. Never excuse yourself.

LET GO OF DISTURBANCES

It is very important to detach ourselves from the distractions or negative thoughts. It's human nature that we tend to get into the past more than the future. The past is over and dead, and we should never worry about these things and always strive to be positive with our thoughts. The best thing about the past is that it educates you for future growth and to not repeat the same mistakes. We should always think forward and not backwards. Life shows only what lies ahead. If you keep looking back while driving the car on the busy highway, there is a good chance you will meet a serious accident. It is as simple as life is. It is too dangerous to keep thinking about the past.

Time spent in hatred is not only wasted, but it changes the thought patterns of the human mind. Thoughts of hatred or negative thoughts do not harm anyone except the person who indulges in them.

The bottom line: There is only a forward direction in life. It is a waste of energy and time to think about the past. Being humans, we're given a true gift of forgetting the things after a specific period of time. You may forget about the things if not immediately but later in the future. If you believe in that, start practicing to let go of all the disturbances and negative things immediately and focus on the future. The time spent on hatred is not only wasted, but it stops you from being productive. It is a great quality to achieve success by detaching ourselves from the undesirable past.

POSITIVE THINKING

I cannot tell you how powerful the practice of positive thinking. It is one of the biggest motivators for me to write this book. Our thoughts create our life. Whatever you think deeply about, day-in and day-out, that are what you're going to manifest. It is only a matter of time. Laws of nature do not understand the difference between positive and negative thoughts. It just manifests your wishes or thoughts. Negative thinking weakens the mind, makes it very stressful and leads to wrong/bad decisions. Some examples of negative thinking: Envy, ego, arrogance, anger, selfishness, fear, and failure.

Positive thinking will have no effect on your life, unless it promotes positive action. A few positive habits:

- ❖ Trust yourself (If you don't, then nobody would)
- ❖ Generate positive energy by performing positive actions
- ❖ Be Fearless; Never worry about intangible things.
- ❖ Welcome the problems and solve them with a great passion
- ❖ Find your own avenues towards happiness
- ❖ Avoid negative people and/or related thoughts
- ❖ Always consider every problem as temporary
- ❖ Make sure to laugh at least a couple of times every day

For every situation you come across, put yourself in another person's position and think what you would do in that particular situation. I guarantee you that, you will get the true answer to most of the situations instantaneously. It is a very powerful technique. Do not react immediately just to satisfy the immediate ego but respond responsibly and tactfully. Positive thinking and forgiveness are the synonyms.

Just to paraphrase a real incident -

When I was in my senior high in India, I was obsessed with our country's famous game, cricket. In fact, I was extremely good at it, and I could win the trophy as the best player in the county/district where I lived. Though I was a good student with my A+ grades, the obsession towards the game of cricket started overriding my grades. I started to pay more attention on the game and, eventually, I neglected my studies. The physical director of games at my school encouraged me to participate in state-level tournaments, and I was so fascinated by the game and used to skip the classes. Since my father and mother never graduated from school, they had a lot of expectations on my studies and its progress. My father came to know through one of my school teachers that I had changed my behavior and was not focusing on my studies. I cannot describe how disappointed my father was on that day. He couldn't resist beating me and gave up on all his expectations he built up for years. It was the first experience (and thank God, the last experience, too) for me to get into a situation such as that. Then I closed myself in my room started thinking why my father had to react in such a bad manner. And immediately, I started questioning myself; what would I do if I put myself in my father position by having a son like me? The answer was very instantaneous: My father was right; I would do the same thing he did to me. I was not very confident that cricket would feed me for an entire lifetime as the success rate is fractions. Hence, I took my father's reaction in a positive manner, and promised myself not to play the game anymore. It's been 15 years, since I either played or watched the game on TV. I forgot all about it and started focusing on my studies, and eventually, I earned my BS and MS in computer science and engineering and passed with distinctions and could secure a first job in a world class company. It's all happened with positive thinking.

A friend of mine started complaining about his job and his compensation. He has been paid the same salary for over 4 years. Recently, he was notified from his employer that, there would be a 40% cut in his next paycheck. He was very much worried. The conversation went like this...

Venu: I understand the situation. Remember, every employer tries to compensate their employees based on their performance and value proposition. Your recent pay cut tells me that, either you're valuation of performance came down or the business is struggling to make the money.

My Friend: Well... I am working much harder than before

Venu: You hard work does not help your employer much but the productivity. Especially in this rocky economy, your employer expects double productivity from you to keep the business going.

My Friend: I am doing my job. I do not care about how the business doing overall...

Venu: Well... that's the point... when you don't know end result in your mind, you are not effective at work. You have to ask yourself a simple question - In what way I am adding true value to my employer. To me, complaining about your employer as same as complaining about yourself. You have to understand why the changes were happening thinking from your side first. If you can come up with innovative ideas or new strategies which would add significant value to your business, I see no reason why your employer would want to cut your salary. In fact, there will be a good possibility that, they would double or triple your salary.

My Friend: Hmmmmm...

Venu: Let me ask you this, "What is the salary you wanted to see in your bank every month?"

My Friend: Well...I wanted to double my salary in every paycheck... My landlord is thinking of increasing the rent (complaining again).

Venu: Do you believe in yourself to double your salary?

My Friend: I wish...

Positive Thinking

Venu: You didn't answer my answer...Do you really believe in yourself to double your salary?

My Friend: I wish...I don't think that will ever happen...

Venu: That's the problem! You answered my question exactly the way I expected. Everybody has too many wishes every day. But that's does not help you anyway. Directly or indirectly you are notifying your mind that, you don't believe in doubling your salary but you wish to happen. Basically, you are contradicting yourself and confusing your mind what to do. Unless you believe in yourself and open the gates with clarity in your mind and take corrective actions to double your salary...nothing happens.

My Friend: WOW... now I know what to do...

Venu: If you understand this theory well, open yourself to see your annual salary in your monthly paycheck and act upon it. Sky is the limit... good luck!

The bottom line: Successful people are always dominated by positive thinking. Never contradict yourself in any matter. Keep a strong gatekeeper in your mind just to allow ONLY positive thoughts. It is like having anti-virus software to protect from viruses on your mind. The things you believe are the things you practice every moment of your life.

FEAR

The most dangerous habits of all - FEAR. Fear comes in many forms; Fear of failure, fear of illness, fear of death, fear of speaking, fear of darkness, fear of some unforeseen things, fear of criticism, etc.

In general, Fear comes in two types which I like to call tangible and intangible. Tangible fear is the obvious stuff. For example, we may be afraid if we are in danger, we may be scared of a dangerous creature or animal, or we may have a fear of someone who we perceive as being stronger or better than ourselves.

Intangible fear, however, is not as clear cut. Intangible fear stops us being the person we really want to be; intangible fear tells us that we can never do the things we have always dreamt of; intangible fear stops us from even dreaming of the things we would like to be or do; intangible fear keeps us in our comfort zone; intangible fear can stop us loving and being loved. Intangible fear can definitely stop us from leading the life we want to lead!

The truth of the matter is intangible fear never exists. It so happened that, many believe something of this kind exists, and they start worrying about it. Hence, you are creating your own problem.

Fear kills the creativity, reduces energy levels, and creates a lot of unnecessary assumptions. Have you ever noticed the most common thing among all successful people in the world is they are fearless? Just ask yourself these questions: Why fear at all? Would there be any advantage keeping fear within you?

This universal law does not understand the difference between the fearful and the strong minded. As per the law of attraction, whatever you believe and conceive that is what you are going to manifest.

Fear of Failure

Fear of failure is one of the greatest fears people have. Fear of failure is closely related to fear of criticism and fear of rejection. Most of the first time entrepreneurs fail because of the 'failure syndrome' in their minds. A lot of people doubt themselves about their future events and anticipate that something is not going to work. If don't see something in real, don't even bother about it. Every failure you come across is the result of the actions performed and it is just a temporary. In reality, there is no failure but only feedback.

Fear of Speaking

I would like to paraphrase a real situation that happened during my college days -

Fear

I went to a public school in a village in India where there was no formal training on interpersonal skills and public speaking, etc. Mostly, I studied in regional language (Telugu Medium) until senior high. I happened to go to a college near my home town where most of what was taught was in a regional language, so I was very much covered there, without much emphasis on English speaking skills. I went on to do masters in computer science & engineering at one of the famous institutes, which happened to be in another state in India. As you may know, every state is different in its own way in India, and they all speak their own regional languages. As part of the master's degree, I was immediately offered a teaching assistance scholarship. Though I enjoyed my scholarships, I was not called for any programs for the first four months. I completely forgot about the teaching assistance too. One fine morning, my professor called on me and asked me to take a class for BS students on one of the computer science engineering subjects that afternoon. It was at 11AM in the morning, and I was asked to take a class at 1PM that same day. You can imagine how a person like me would feel like; though I am good at the subject, I cannot speak English fluently. I cannot tell you how I felt at that moment. It was like a train riding at 1000 miles per hour in my heart. I had no clue how I could handle that situation at that moment. I was very comfortable having a one-to-one assistance session but definitely not in a group. With all these tensions, I went into the cafeteria, and sat at the table thinking deeply about the situation. There were a lot of things flowing freely into the mind, like: What if I fail in this assistance session? Do they cancel my scholarship? How can I win the hearts of the sixty students in the class?

Guess what? My professor stepped into the cafeteria and said, "Hey, Venu! Are you ready for the session this afternoon?" "Of course not," I said to myself. I wouldn't dare to tell my professor. In reality, I was not even close to wanting to take the class at that second. I wanted to ask my professor if I could take the class at a later point of time. Again I asked myself, 'what if he says take the class tomorrow?' There is no way to escape. My gut feeling guided me to go forward without thinking about short-term alternatives. I had no other choice. I said to my professor, "Yes sir, I am ready to take the class this afternoon." Then the professor went to the line to get a meal. It was 12:15PM in the afternoon. My professor shares the table with me, and asks, "Have you ever taken this class before?" and I said "Absolutely. I did many times, Sir."

While we were talking, Joseph, one of the class leads from the electronics engineering departments noticed my professor and joined us at the table. Joseph said they didn't have any other classes in the afternoon as one of their professors was sick. My professor asked Joseph if the electronics engineering class would participate in the same class which I am going to lead the same afternoon. I asked Joseph "How many of you guys are in the class?" Joseph said there was about forty. It was like I was very close to having a heart attack at that moment. "Oh my God, another 40 students, which totals 100?" I had no other choice but to strengthen my will power. After a couple of minutes, I closed my eyes, and I said to myself:

"...whatever is going to happen to will happen. Why should I worry about this? It is not a big deal. I am sure there were a lot of people like me would have faced this kind of challenge before and

overcome through it. If they could do it, I can do it too. Why worry? I am ready to take any criticism."

That's it. It was the great realization for me. I had no idea where these words came from. However, it helped me in a big way. While I was getting deep insight from myself at that time, my professor interrupted me and asked, "Would you be able to give me a pitch on what you are going to talk about in the class?" I could explain him very confidently on the subject for about 5 minutes. Those moments gave me a lot of confidence in myself at that moment. Since I could talk to my professor successfully, I told myself, "Let me take the class just by looking at the professor's eyes and focus on the subject". Unfortunately, my wish couldn't last for more than 5 minutes. My professor got a call from his boss and said to me that he won't to be able to attend the class, and he asked me to proceed. Finally, I stepped into the classroom with almost one hundred students. I happened to find a lady with beautiful eyes in the class, and I started the class by looking at her eyes. It was very embarrassing for the lady, but I had no choice. I had no idea what the other students thought of me, and I had not changed my focus, and it went for about ten minutes nonstop. Interestingly enough, I started enjoying the session with the big group of people for the first time. The lady I was looking at changed her focus to the board, and I slowly switched my focus into another lady sitting next to her. I was going nonstop now. I immediately realized, "Bingo... Something is working here." I said to myself, 'change the attention towards the rest of the crowd'. I kept on shifting my focus on the entire class. It was a fantastic experience for me. That was the big realization for me in many ways which I couldn't explain. As I explained, you can imagine how I remembered every moment of that day.

At the end of the session, I offered students a "Q&A." I had no other choice but turning my eyes to different locations wherever a question arose. It increased my self-confidence. I very well exceeded my own expectations for the first time. It was like a big ocean flowing through me freely. Ever since I mastered the art of teaching, I now only teach big groups of people, and I do not like small groups any more.

If you observe closely, I had never given up on the situation even though I was not capable of taking the class initially. Life gives you bigger and bigger challenges. If you can resolve the situations tactfully, life gives you even bigger challenges. You should never give up on any situation; always strive hard to prove yourself. If there is any criticism just welcome it. That's how life makes you stronger and successful in whatever you do. There is no place for losers in the success world.

Fear of Death

I read many articles about those who were close to death and turned out to be the most successful people after losing the 'fear of the death syndrome'. Take look at the real life incident of William Wang, Founder of TV-maker Vizio.

William Wang understands keeping things in perspective. As one of 96 survivors aboard Singapore Airlines 747 that took off from the wrong runway in Taiwan, which struck a construction site and broke in two, Wang instantly realized that the difficulties of his various technology businesses weren't such a big deal--not when

Fear

83 passengers and crew members were killed that day in 2000. Wang shut down all his businesses after the crash, and in 2003 got into the flat-screen TV business by launching Vizio. His idea was to combine low prices with high quality and exceptional customer support, and to make this approach profitable through extremely lean operations. Wang, started the company with $600,000, and Vizio generates more than $2 billion in sales.

I will tell you this: We're living in a world where nothing is guaranteed other than our strengths and beliefs. What is the guarantee that we get home safely from work on a freeway, regardless of how good a driver you are? What is the guarantee that you have a safe flight/train/bus on your travel? What is the guarantee not to have any unknown floods/earthquakes/hurricanes, etc? Do you have any control over them? Absolutely not. Then why fear something which is not a reality yet?

Just live happily every moment as it comes and never worry about the things where you have no control.

Fear of Criticism

If you think that, others may criticize you for doing things which you like the most puts you in a great depression. If you have a fear of criticism, you are stopping your growth at the cost of your own happiness but life does not appreciate that. In reality, no one has time to think about your acts. Even if they do, it is only a temporary. Follow your heart in all matters without hurting others and their opinions.

One Book for Life Success

I would like to share some quotes written by Mother Theresa. For those of you who do not know Mother Theresa, here is a short bio (Excerpts from Wikipedia):

Mother Theresa (August 26, 1910 – September 5, 1997) was born on August 26, 1910, in Skopje, now the capital of the Republic of Macedonia. She arrived in India in 1929, and began her novitiate in Darjeeling, near the Himalayan Mountains in India. She then founded the Missionaries of Charity in Kolkata (Calcutta), India in 1950. For over 45 years she ministered to the poor, sick, orphaned, and dying, while guiding the Missionaries of Charity's expansion, first throughout India and then in other countries. By the 1970s, she had become internationally famed as a humanitarian and advocate for the poor and helpless, due in part to documentary, and book, Something Beautiful for God by Malcolm Muggeridge. She won the Nobel Peace Prize in 1979 and India's highest civilian honor, the Bharat Ratna, in 1980 for her humanitarian work.

Here are the wonderful quotes from Mother Theresa...

People are often unreasonable, illogical and self-centered.
Forgive them anyway.

If you are kind, people may accuse you of selfish motives;
Be kind anyway.

If you are successful, you will win some false friends and some true enemies;
Succeed anyway.

Fear

If you are honest and frank, people may cheat you;
Be honest and frank anyway.

What you spend years building, someone could destroy overnight;
Build anyway.

If you find serenity and happiness, they may be jealous;
Be happy anyway.

The good you do today, people will often forget tomorrow;
Do well anyway.

Give the world the best you have, and it may never be enough;
Give the world the best you have anyway.

You see, in the final analysis, it is between you and God;
It never was between you and them anyway.

~Mother Teresa~

The bottom line: When you are fearless, you are free from the outer world and your self-confidence levels would increase tremendously. Never allow anything to come to your mind other than your immediate priorities and/or goals. You have no time to think about unproductive things, especially 'intangible fear'. Just follow your heart and do whatever you love the most, and never worry about others and their criticisms. A person cannot be an absolute failure unless he/she permits fear into his/her mind.

RISK TAKING

We live in an era where no risk means no rewards. If you believe in your ability to create something new or construct a new idea, you do not need to quit your current job and focus on that immediately. Before you take any risk, do thorough research on your strengths, beliefs, passions, industry, and share the same with your trusted friends and see what they would think of it, and get their sincere feedback. Once you're clear with the vision and basic plan, and the decent financing, you don't need to wait, just start. At the same time, you should have a reserve to meet the basic necessities for the next five to six months without banking on the immediate profits from the new business. Some people get excited about their idea and quit their current jobs and start something on their own. It has its own pros and cons. The basic reasons why most of the first-time entrepreneurs fail – Not enough funds; No proper planning; Not able to persist; Not able to take rejections; Fear of failure; One man army; Doing everything in rush.

The bottom line: Most of them prefer to take the easier way out, because they don't want to take risks and they cannot accept failures. However, great risk often leads to great rewards. When there is no risk, there is no reward. However, an intensive planning and readiness to the war are very much required before you proceed.

PERSISTENCE

The best habit of human nature is PERSISTENCE. There is nothing to replace the word "Persistence." It is human nature that we all tend to make mistakes knowingly or unknowingly. The most important thing is learning from the past mistakes and realizing in a positive manner to achieve the desired results. There is a process for everything we come across in our lives. You can always expedite the process in comparison to others if you can understand the game plan well. The baby cannot walk on the floor when he or she is first born. He or she needs a lot of practice for a number of months. How many times have you seen a baby strive hard to walk even though they're not able to stand on their feet at their early stage? Even after failing multiple times, the baby does not give up and he or she will practice it repeatedly with more enthusiasm. The same rule applies for any situation and keeps you doing the same things in different and unique ways until you achieve the desired results. Failure is a part of the game, it is not the destination.

There is a nice story about the frog in a milk-pail...

A frog was hopping around a farmyard, when it decided to investigate the barn. Being somewhat careless, and maybe a little too curious, he ended up falling into a pail half-filled with fresh milk. As he swam about attempting to reach the top of the pail, he found that the sides of the pail were too high and steep to reach. He tried to stretch his back legs to push off the bottom of the pail but found it too deep. But this frog was determined not to give up, and he continued to struggle. He kicked and squirmed and kicked and squirmed, until at last, all his churning about in the milk had turned the milk into a big hunk of butter. The butter was now solid enough for him to climb onto and get out of the pail! "Never Give Up!"

Probably, the greatest example of persistence is Abraham Lincoln (16th President of United States). If you want to learn about somebody who didn't quit, look at no further. Born into poverty, Lincoln was faced with defeat throughout his life. He lost eight elections, twice failed in business and suffered a nervous breakdown. He could have quit many times - but he didn't, and because he didn't quit, he became one of the greatest presidents in the history of United States of America. Lincoln was a champion and he never gave up.

Here is a sketch of Lincoln's road to the White House:

* 1816 - His family was forced out of their home. He had to work to support them.
* 1818 - His mother died.
* 1831 - Failed in business.
* 1832 - Ran for the state legislature - lost.
* 1832 - Also lost his job - wanted to go to law school but couldn't get in.
* 1833 - Borrowed some money from a friend to begin a business and by the end of the year he was bankrupt. He spent the next 17 years of his life paying off this debt.

34

Persistance

* 1834 - Ran for the state legislature again - won.
* 1835 - Was engaged to be married, sweetheart died and his heart was broken.
* 1836 - Had a total nervous breakdown and was in bed for six months.
* 1838 - Sought to become speaker of the state legislature - defeated.
* 1840 - Sought to become elector - defeated.
* 1843 - Ran for Congress - lost.
* 1846 - Ran for Congress again - this time he won - went to Washington and did a
good job.
* 1848 - Ran for re-election to Congress - lost.
* 1849 - Sought the job of land officer in his home state - rejected.
* 1854 - Ran for Senate of the United States - lost.
* 1856 - Sought the Vice-Presidential nomination at his party's national convention –
get less than 100 votes.
* 1858 - Ran for U.S. Senate again - again he lost.
* 1860 - Elected president of the United States.

It took Abraham Lincoln thirty years to achieve his dream of becoming the President of the United States. Do not be discouraged if you have tried and tried and still haven't achieved your dreams yet. Worthwhile goals and aspirations will always take time to accomplish. However, you can achieve them for sure with your sincere effort and great persistence.

The bottom line: Successful people never ever quit. Always try one more time until you succeed.

BEING NICE

Being nice creates a lot of miracles in both personal and professional lives. Niceness comes in the forms of: Having a good smile, saying "thank you", showing gratitude, appreciating others, helping others without expecting anything in return, listening to others attentively, and so on. Little things ONLY matter. There are no big things without the summation of little things.

It takes only 30 seconds to form an impression on other's attitudes. The moment you show any pride, arrogance, ego, jealousy, non-verbal signs (body language), superiority to others, you create an immediate bad mark in other's minds. It sometimes creates long term enemies, too. You're directly responsible for your behavior and acts. It takes every moment to build the character around the people in any given environment. However, it takes only a single moment to ruin the same character with any bad acts. Being nice to others pays back in a big way. Especially when you engaged in a business conversation, you have to be even more careful.

We make calls to customer service centres when we need any help. It is very understandable that the volume of calls they handle in a day is humongous and every customer service representative gets overwhelmed with the number of calls they receive. I have had both good and bad experiences as many of you may have had.

Some of the representatives are extremely polite on the phone and greet you well and listen to the issues with utmost care, and they attempt to resolve the problem in the best way possible. Some of them get irritated at times, it might be because of many reasons; they're too tired answering multiple calls and handling similar kinds of situations with different people all day long. Apparently, every customer being concerned about his/her own needs always want to get warm responses from representatives.

If we come across a bad representative on the phone, we immediately create an impression about the business rather than the person we talked to. I come across many of the situations where some of my friends say "Oh, their customer service is awful." It does not matter how many times they had the best customer service with the same business in the past. Only the bad experiences come into the lime light so quickly. In reality, though, it is one representative create the bad mark, and not the business. You can imagine how dangerous these kinds of impressions are to growth of any business.

I once happened to talk to a representative, which happened to be her first day on the job, and she made me wait longer time than usual. Though I was not comfortable spending too much time to resolve a small issue, the lady was very polite and nice throughout our conversation. At the end of the call, she admitted to herself that it took longer than usual, and she promised to serve faster next time (though we never know who we get next time). That left me with a good impression.

Being Nice

The bottom line: Being nice would not only make others happy but the entire environment. It is the most powerful technique to achieve better results in our day-2-day lives. Never burn the bridges in your personal as well as professional lives permanently. When you start being nice, the entire environment wins!

JEALOUSY

Jealousy is a negative emotion. Many people feel jealous time to time. Jealousy comes in the forms of - envying about others' success; benchmarking with the immediate environment constantly; feeling inferior and insecure; low/extreme self-esteem and so on. People with a strong jealous mindset cannot achieve any bigger goals in their lives. The very the reason being, they tend to compare or benchmark every situation with the immediate environment. The only good thing about being jealous about something - it alerts you to what you want and what is important to you and learn good things from others' achievements.

We need to learn the good from others if they're good in some matters. What is it that we achieve by benchmarking the people who sit next to us in similar career levels and make about the same amount of money? Jealousy ruins both personal as well as professional relationships, and leaves negative thoughts about other people. All these thoughts are not going to be of any use in anyone's personal growth. Every one of us has a space to grow in our own way in this world. We cannot stop anyone's personal growth with a jealous feeling. We need to admit the facts of our strengths and weaknesses and always appreciate others.

Just accept the environment as it is and encourage others to grow and seek help if needed. If one of your friends is successful in his career or business, indirectly, your friend is helping you out to think bigger and create a success of your own. Always consider every situation positively never allow jealousy into the mind. It is just a waste of time.

The bottom line: Never benchmark with your immediate environment. You cannot stop someone's growth by displaying jealousy vice versa. In fact, jealousy plants lot of bad seeds in your mind and lead you to unhappiness. If you're in an investment sector, try to benchmark with Warren Buffet. If you're in a technology industry, try to benchmark with Microsoft or the Google founders. If you're in a real estate business, try to benchmark with Donald Trump and the list goes on and on. Replace the word "Jealousy" with "Inspiration" in your mental dictionary. It really helps you to think and achieve big.

FORGIVENESS

Forgiveness plays a crucial role in our lives by letting go of the past and move forward towards our desired goals. You might have come across a bad person, bad relationship, bad employment or a bad situation. Just forgive them with a positive attitude. There is nothing permanent in this world. Every situation is temporary. Why disturb yourself with thinking about something, which has already happened? The past teaches us what is good and what is bad in the situations we came across. Your job is to not repeat the same mistakes you made in the past and follow the good practices as life comes. Life has only a forward direction (Present -> Future). We cannot replay the past. The past is over, and dead. We have to let go of the past, and allow ourselves to move into the future consciously. It makes you feel very light if you can absorb the technique of forgiveness into your mind.

If someone abuses you or makes undesirable remarks out of anger, then instead of feeling bad about that person, just consider that the person was upset or the person was still not fully matured or accept that you yourself would react in the same way if you put yourself in another person's position. It is not wise to develop any desire for revenge or malice against others. Just remove all the bad memories which you acquired from the past. Forgiveness is a powerful tool, and it makes you feel really good at every situation you come across.

The bottom line: Every situation we across in our lives is a temporary. Whatever the situation you are in today will disappear in couple of minutes or days or weeks or months. Let it go now and move on.

EGO

People with big egos are extremely difficult to get along with. They can be more demanding, self-centered, hostile, and are more likely to let others down. Most of the egotistic people crave for their own personal image, always feeling superior to other people, and they cannot tolerate criticism or disrespect. These people are incredibly demanding, and never accept other's opinions.

When you're a child you would have a lot of innocence about you. As you grow, you tend to accumulate and inherit a lot of things from immediate family, friends, day to day thoughts and actions, relatives, teachers, mentors, peers, employers, and the list goes on and on. With all these previous observations and experiences, you tend to set some guidelines to yourself and create an image called "I." All these acquisitions (could be good or bad or a mix of both) create a self-belief system. Whenever there is a disagreement with others against the one's belief system, ego kicks in. Since you have a strong "I" factor in your system, that's where your ego resides. How many times we would have come across these directly or indirectly:

"I" am the richest person in the whole community; I hardly see any people around on par with my status;

"I" am the creator of this big corporation; None of my friends were as successful as me

"I" am the great scientist in this field; No one else could do it; I am the only answer;

"I" am the most beautiful person in our university; Most people around me are ugly looking;

"I" am the genius in my class; The rest are all dumb;

"I" am the star sales person in the company; No one even comes close to the targets achieved by me;

"I" own a big mansion valued at multi-million dollars; Most of my relatives are still renting and cannot even afford a house;

"I" helped you in many ways; You better respect me always;

If you ever pay deep attention on this single letter word, "I," you would understand more about your true nature without considering any external influences. What is this "I?" There is no greater accomplishment ever made in the history without a group of masterminds. Absolutely, there is nothing wrong in having a high self-esteem, intentions to acquire more wealth, creating a brand for yourself, enjoying luxuries, etc., But it is not wise to underestimate others by comparing them with your current status. If you are very successful today, then chances are you were not always that way. Success and failures are not permanent in our lives. If you show modest and kind behavior to others when you're successful, the energy will keep you in the same position or maybe will allow you to achieve even more success.

The letter "E" in ego stands for "Enemy". Ego creates more enemies in contrast to friends. In fact, ego is the core factor of human sufferings. You need more people who can support and encourage you in all matters, but you do not need enemies. The more enemies you have, the more energy gets drained from you, and you become an enemy to others, too.

The bottom line: Never allow ego into your life. You create more enemies with your ego. You can attract more people in your life without an ego. Nothing is bigger than happiness.

GREED

There is nothing available for free in this world. You need to make every effort to acquire wealth, success, happiness, and prosperity. There are no legal shortcuts to achieve success. If you win a lottery, the excitement lasts only for a couple of months. If you make money by doing any wrong things, the compound interests start from that moment and get accumulated as a debt you have to repay along with the interest in one form or another in the future.

Just remember this small quote, " Easy come and Easy go."

You will have tremendous satisfaction if you pay your bills with your hard earned money using your own skills.

How many times we would hear about some of the most brilliant and successful people in the corporate world being sent to jail for participating in fraudulent activities. It is always good to have right intentions to acquire success in a right manner, and to not just look for shortcuts.

The Bottom Line: We come into this world with empty hands and leave the same way with no exceptions. All it matters - How good a person you are with your family and society in between.

PERFECTION

Perfection comes with progressive steps towards achieving desired outcomes. There are few things in this world that are really perfect. We need to learn the habit of adjusting with what we have while moving towards our goal rather than expecting perfection right away. In the early years of our lives, we learn and practice the "baby steps" multiple times before we're able to walk without any additional support. It takes only one second to give up on anything. If you have a great business plan, start with what you have rather than expecting to find full funds in your bank account and stellar teams on the board. Every process takes its own time. Perfection is the process of getting better every day-- it is not the destination. Just start with what you have. If you have a good plan, then perfection follows automatically.

The Bottom Line: Perfection consists not in doing extraordinary things, but in doing ordinary things extraordinarily well.

SMALL THINGS MATTER

Small things have big results. Our job is to deliver each and everything in the best way possible, regardless of whether it is small or big. We can always prioritize the tasks to be done in a certain order on any given day. Once you commit to perform any task, it should be the best of your knowledge, and you should stick to the timelines.

You have to be very cautious about accepting tasks and successfully delivering the best results possible. In today's competitive world, we tend to work on multiple things at once without having much focus on a specific task. That's where the productivity suffers. It is wonderful to multi task, but there should not be any deviations from the priorities you committed to deliver.

If you complete a task effectively, it will energize your confidence and satisfaction levels to achieve even more. The best regard for good work is more work. More work equals more personal growth and success.

Bottom Line: Every small thing matters in order to achieve big thing.

ANGER

Some people strongly believe that there is no way they can make other people understand their emotions and feelings during hard times without displaying anger. It is human nature that we tend to get into the anger mode when we are unable to accept or digest any unfavorable things. There is nothing wrong with being angry once in a while. The good part is it gives you a bit of relief. However, the bad part is it drains a lot of your positive energy, and it can create negativity in your mind. In fact, the anger makes the mind weaker. While we are angry, whatever decisions we make at that moment will not be very effective. We need to explain these things that are bothering us to others in a more natural way and calmly. Sometimes we lose respect for other people by showing bad temper frequently. If you get into the anger mode, just think of a beautiful baby smiling and moving in the cradle for few seconds or count from one to ten, and ask yourself to slow down and reanalyze the situation and respond accordingly. Try to use whichever technique you are comfortable with, and come out of the anger mode as quickly as possible and practice the same method repeatedly. At the same time, if you come across a situation where other people are taking advantage of you, then just avoid them.

The Bottom Line: For every minute you are angry, you lose sixty seconds of happiness. Therefore, it is not worth it.

WELCOME PROBLEMS
FOR A BETTER LIFE

Look at every situation you come across in your life as a chance to change for the better. Some of the situations like: You're about to get laid off from your job, losing money on a business venture, being in a bad relationship, financial crisis, your children's education, and the list goes on and on…

Being a true human being, you should be prepared to handle any kind of situation with a great ease. There is no problem exists in this world without a solution. Lock has no meaning without a key. They (Problem and solution) always born together. If fact, if you think deep, you can find multiple solutions for the same problem and choose the best one.

Every problem teaches you a good lesson and makes you stronger than before. Every problem allows you to grow personally, mentally, and spiritually. If life is that simple, we would be sitting on the beach and partying every day for a lifetime. You have a purpose in your life, the universe creates challenges for you to overcome and to help you understand who you truly are. You need to look at every problem with optimism and lean towards solving the problems in the most efficient way. If you ever observe your past, I guarantee you that, you would see how you've handled many challenges tactfully. If you could overcome those challenges in the past, then no doubt you can do the same in the future, too. No problem is larger than your life. Why worry about problems? Let's welcome the problems and enjoy solving them and keep progressing towards your personal growth and success.

The bottom line: Every problem opens new doors for your life betterments. Solve them with a great passion and ask for even more. It is the only way to groom yourself.

BE A STUDENT FOR LIFE

To remain competent in today's fast growing world, you need to keep abreast with all the latest developments in the areas of your employment and interests. The information is overwhelming: Internet, TV, books, conferences, events, and so on. All it needs is curiosity and time to learn and upgrade yourself every single day. If you can sincerely allocate a specific time for self-improvement (thirty minutes to an hour or more), I guarantee you that you are on your way to your personal growth and success.

It is never too late to learn more and receive more training on a subject of interest and go to school to upgrade yourself. For example, if you're a store manager and wanted to move up the ladder, do a business administration course. If you're very serious, then there are lots of ways to get trained these days, such as personal observation, online training, etc. There are tremendous benefits for being a lifetime student. Your job is directly proportionate to your educational background, skill set, experience and track record. Always seek to improve your skills. The more you learn new things, the more confident you will be in the society and corporate environment.

The bottom line: You can lose everything you acquired in your entire life but not your education, knowledge, wisdom, experience, and self-confidence.

HELP OTHERS

Helping others should be unconditional. Some people have good hearts and like to help others, but they expect pay backs when needed. That is not a true helper. Once the help is extended you need to detach yourself from it. If you ever observe your past experiences close enough and ask yourself, "Was there anyone who helped me in the past?". Then you would probably notice that a lot of different people have helped you; Parents, friends, teachers, peers, professors, mentors, and so on. If you get motivated by someone's speech, then of course, you got the help. You should thank all of these people--whoever extended that help directly or indirectly in your life. Due to many limitations, you don't always get an opportunity to go back and help all those people who helped you since your childhood days.

Unfortunately, there are lots of people who believe their lives are struck with bad luck, because they are not able to make ends meet or are trying too hard to make a living or lost a job, and so on. If you have real intentions of helping other people, then do it unconsciously. Life is like a river that flows in a circular fashion. The more you help others the better comes to you.

If you lend material things such as money, you can always expect others to pay you back. If you extend the help in the forms used value, such as advice, mentoring, inspiring, motivating, and showing the alternative ways for their personal growth would actually a bigger help than lending money. Extending help in terms of non-material things is not an investment to save and expect returns with the interest later. It should be purely unconditional.

I once met a man named John in an airport who looked like he had almost lost his hopes in finding a job. John told me he was on a job hunt for more than four months, and was unable to get through with it. I spent almost thirty minutes with him identifying his areas of improvement, and recommended a couple of agencies that I knew. He was very excited and he hugged me at the end of our discussion. I couldn't leave my business card with him because I had to rush to get on my flight. After a couple of weeks, I happened to run into John in another town where he was placed on a job. He mentioned that he approached an agency which I recommended could find a job within a week's time. He offered to take me to lunch on the same day. I told him that I didn't expect anything from him in return when we spoke again. All I requested of him was if he finds any needy people who might be looking for jobs, to try and help them out and ask them to help others in return. He promised me that he will do just that whenever possible. That was the only thing that I expected from him in return.

If everyone (whoever makes a decent living) can donate at least 0.25% of their annual earnings towards eradicating world poverty, we can see a better world with no poverty in less than 50 years. Donating 0.25% of your net worth in your life time would not make much impact for your ancestry. For example: If you make $40,000 per annum, donating $100 towards trusted charities and foundations would add a great value to the society. If not money,

Help Others

help others in terms of mentoring, motivating, inspiring, training, finding job and anything that would improve their current living standards.

Helping others unconditionally is the greatest feeling in the world. If you help someone at any capacity guess what happens? You will get help from someone in one form or another. It is a cycle.

We are fortunate enough to have some of the kindest people on earth donating their fortune to philanthropic causes. Just to name a few of these kind people: Warren Buffet (one of the top 5 richest people in the world) gives away most of his fortune to the Gates Foundation. Bill Gates donated most of his wealth to his own foundation and joined the foundation full-time to improve health conditions across the world. Their foundation's activities, internationally famous, are focused on world health -- fighting such diseases as malaria, HIV/AIDS, and tuberculosis -- and on improving U.S. libraries and high schools. Mother Theresa dedicated her entire life to helping people in Calcutta, India. The list goes on and on...

All these people will be admired for centuries for their great help towards society.

The bottom line: Do not expect returns for any help you extend to others. The only help you should expect in return is asking the ones you helped to help others in a similar way. There is nothing worse than a selfish living in this world. It makes you feel really good when you help others.

DECISION MAKING

Everyone has their own views and opinions on certain things based on their own experiences and influences. Every individual possesses his/her unique talent, skills, strengths and weaknesses. There is nothing called perfect in this world. If there is one, it is just an individual's perception. Some people attempt to impose their own personal opinions on you. You understand yourself better than any else one in the world. If you find true value (beyond your current knowledge) in others' suggestions, there should not be any second thoughts, just accept it. Being stubborn closes many doors and stunts your personal growth and sometimes creates enemies, too. You have to see things through other's points of view to make the world a better place. It is always nice to listen and seek other opinions and suggestions. However, you have to be wise enough to accept those suggestions and customize them to your personal outlook.

The process should be something like this: ask (yourself / others)-> Receive -> Trust -> Test -> Execute.

The bottom line: Your success rate depends on how fast you can make the best decisions and act upon them.

THINKING IN OTHER'S PERSPECTIVE

We come across many different people and situations in our day to day lives. It is true that many of us are big fans of ourselves. We tend to get into arguments if we feel we're disrespected, and if we see something that happens to offend our personal beliefs. Most people tend to think irrationally or be closed minded without considering the entire situation.

I strongly believe that most of the arguments you usually get into will be avoided if you start analyzing the situation more closely than ever by asking yourself a simple question: "How would I react if I were in other person's position?"

Nothing happens automatically, and there is a reason for everything. If your manager yells at you at work for not being able to perform well, admit to yourself that you would do the same if you're a manager having an employee like you. You have to quest for positive things in the situation rather than building revenge against the manager.

If you will observe, most of the mature people never worry about petty things, they always focus on the big picture. Ask yourself these sincere questions: "How many times have I come across bad tempers in the past?"; "Did they add any value to my life?" I am sure you would agree now that these petty things are just a waste of time.

These kinds of situations will ruin your peace of mind and create a negative mentality against others. It is very easy to say something bad about others. Many people think it comes without consequence. In reality, this is not true. Thinking badly about others will lead you nowhere, while creating a selfish creature-yourself. Always try to think good about others. Should you come across any negative people, just ignore them. Never allow negativity into your mind, and make sure you have no room for tempers and negative feelings.

The computer acts pretty much the same as our minds. The more junk and viruses you have on your computer, the less performance it offers, and sometimes it acts weird and starts deleting the good stuff. You need to have a gate keeper to your mind like having a licensed copy of an anti-virus program on your computer. The gatekeeper to your mind should just be your consciousness.

There are only two simple ways to have peace of mind.

- ❖ Take every situation as positively as possible and think about how it could benefit you in the future.
- ❖ Avoid confrontational situations.

The bottom line: Whatever the situation you come across, instead of reacting instantly, trust your own feelings and also think deep enough through others' perspective and respond tactfully. Do not deliver anything, if you cannot accept the same voice from others.

NEVER STOP YOUR LIFE

Many people stop at times or at least slow down in their lives when they are upset because of any unpleasant situation. The cause might be: financial crisis; loss of job; annoying comments by someone; some insult; bitter criticism from somewhere; abusive boss; the list goes on and on.

Whatever bad situations we deal with in our lives is just temporary. When we come out of those situations, our life will once again go back to its usual pace, but the loss of time in the transition period is a permanent loss. Just ask yourself a few questions: "How many times were I in an oblivious state in the past?", "Did I get anything positive out of that situation?" and "Do I care about that situation now?"

Now, you really do not pay much attention to some bad situations that you came across in your life. You are very busy with new events you come across in your day to day life. If not immediately, you will definitely forget about those bad situations a week or a month or a year later. The past is over and dead, and you learned your lesson: Do not repeat the same mistakes again. If this is so, why disturb yourself with any situation when it is almost guaranteed that you will not care about it later in the future. You may think it is hard to get out of unpleasant situations, but force yourself using your will power and never distract the tempo of your mind.

The bottom line: Whenever you come across any disappoint moments in your life, just ask yourself these simple questions - "Is this a cyclone or thunderstorm or hurricane or tsunami?"; "Am I the first person to face this challenge in this world?". When you believe that you are larger than the problem, you can fix any problem with a greater ease in no time. Life should flow like a river with no interruption. Dry rivers do not impress anyone.

COMMUNICATION

From the moment, you wake up in the morning until you go to bed at night, all you do is communicate with others or within the self. Communication skills are difficult yet important to understand, and we need to strive hard to keep our communication powerful, effective, and leave good impressions on others. Our communication is truly a blueprint for our behavior. It is a universal truth that, it takes only a few seconds to get an initial impression of a person you meet based on their communication skills. If you want to be a student for life in one area, learn to improve your communication skills effectively every day.

Effective communication is all about conveying your messages to other people clearly and unambiguously. It's also about receiving information that others are sending to you with as little distortion as possible. The best forms of communication can be one of the following: verbal, body language, facial expressions, eye contact, gestures, mannerisms, and even silence. Research says 80% of communication is nonverbal. Most failures in business or personal relationships are failures in communication.

Some of the positive signs of communication:

- ❖ Listen! Listen! Listen Actively!
- ❖ Have a smile

- ❖ Show respect
- ❖ Show enthusiasm
- ❖ Greet others unconditionally
- ❖ Be curious and honest
- ❖ Try not to interrupt when other person talks unless there is an emergency
- ❖ Be aware of body gestures and constant eye contact
- ❖ Observe the surroundings and react
- ❖ Stick to positive communication
- ❖ Use plain language and brief (Avoid over-talking unless the situation demands)
- ❖ Never show pride or arrogance
- ❖ Watch your temper levels
- ❖ Offer advice only when asked
- ❖ When you deal with business matters, keep an eye on the clock and adjust the conversation accordingly
- ❖ Appreciate others in front of group of people; If there is any criticism involved, it should be one-2-one only
- ❖ The best sound for any person in the world is his/her *name*. Use person's name during the conversation (whenever appropriate)

There are lots of tools available to record the conversations today. Try to record the conversations you participated in and listen to them multiple times and see if there is any room for the improvement. You will be amazed at how many things you can learn about your communication when you listen to your own voice over and over. If you're honest with yourself, you will not find any better critic other than you. Remember, practice is what makes the difference in your life.

Communication

The bottom line: Most of all, listening is a very important thing yet powerful skill during any conversation. It is human nature that people tend to talk more about themselves. Based on the situation, allow the lead person(s) to talk more about them, and you keep listening. People get attracted to good listeners and create a good impression instantly. If you want to get appreciated from others, you have to appreciate them first. Especially, when you deal with business matters, listen to your own inner voice before you deliver and think how the listener(s) would react to it in their perspective and change your inner voice to create a significant impact if needed and then deliver. It does not matter how long you had a conversation with other parties – All it matter is how much impact you created by the end of the conversation. Rest all follows automatically. Great communication should be two-way, simple, precise, and clear.

EDUCATION IS NEVER ENOUGH

Education only gets you the first job or an entry into the field. After that, all it matters is - Your imagination, wisdom, skills, experiences, observations, commitment towards the life, determination, and fearless nature. If every MBA graduate from the top business schools (i.e., Harvard, Stanford, Wharton, London Business, INSEAD etc), becomes an entrepreneur, we should have at least Fortune million companies not just a Fortune 500 in the world.

According to Forbes, more than 20% of the self-made American billionaires on the most recent list of the World's Billionaires 2009 have either never started or never completed college. This is especially true of those destined for careers as technology entrepreneurs: Bill Gates (Microsoft), Steve Jobs (Apple), Michael Dell (Dell), Larry Ellison (Oracle), and Theodore Waitt (Gateway).

I would like to share with you a real situation....

Once there was a software development manager, who was reporting to me when I was working as an executive in a software development firm. I had to rate him once in every 6 months as part of the appraisal process based on his performance and accomplishments to promote him to next level and raise his compensation level. He had a master's degree from one of the top universities from US. But I was not so impressed with his performance considering the feedback from the customer and team. When I rated him with "C" ("A" being the highest), he questioned me " I have graduated from one of the top schools and been working here for more than 7 years. Why is my rating so low?". I told him that, "You may have been working for 7 years with a master's degree from a top school, but it does count as you are producing the results like an employee who has just been working for one year, but you repeat the one year experience for 7 times. You never learn any new things. That's why I rated you with 'C'". Though he irritated instantly and left that place, it took him couple of days to realize what I was talking about. Later, he came back to me and apologized for his acts and promised me to change his attitude and produce more results.

Another situation which I came across…

A friend of mine who lost his momentum being in the same job for over 14 years asked my advice going for an MBA. He told me that he spent almost 2 years thinking about this. Indeed, I was very happy for him that, he realized the importance of his professional life at the age of 35. At the same time, I was not sure about his future plans. First of all, he had no savings whatsoever counting on every paycheck and a family to feed. He was thinking of going for $100,000 student loan. I asked him if the MBA was a necessary for him considering all of his circumstances. I also made it clear that, it would take at least 3 years to complete part-time MBA course and takes another 3-4 years to pay off the debt. By that time, he will be at his 40. Though I know the importance of an MBA, instead, I suggested him to read some leadership/management/inspirational *book, attend groups, personal development seminars and start looking at the big picture within the same organization, wherever he works. I asked him to start thinking/acting like his boss from that moment onwards. I also asked him to make a promise to his family that, he is going to create some change in their lives within 3 months. He is doing much better than ever now.*

The bottom line: Education only gets you the first job. After that - your abilities, skill set, experience, hard work, performance, wisdom, innovation, results - are what matters to move you up to the ladder. If you want to achieve something new, announce the same along with the timeline to your family, friends and loved ones much before you start work on it. This kind of action will ignite you to achieve the desired result much before the committed date. The most important factors to achieve any success in life are commitment and promise.

RELATIONSHIP

Having a harmonious relationship is the greatest gift anybody would ever get from life. There is an old saying that goes, "Win the hearts at home first before conquer the outer world." Unfortunately, there are lots of couples fighting for nothing other than satisfying their egos today. We hear most of the complaints or blames in one of the following forms:

- ❖ He/She is not intelligent enough to handle the situation.
- ❖ He/She is too lazy.
- ❖ He/She constantly criticizes.
- ❖ He/She never smiles, and is always angry.
- ❖ He/She is not affectionate and never in a good mood.
- ❖ He/She is not good looking.

The list goes on and on…

There is no problem existing in this world without any permanent fix or solution. Most of everyone is looking for easy routes rather than finding the right solutions to resolve their issues. Easy routes give only temporary relief, and people come across the same problem repeatedly until they find the permanent fix to the problem. It is so unfortunate that a lot of people are so selfish in today's world.

I would like to share a couple of situations which I have come across…

I met a nice couple in Los Angeles a few years back. I happened to know the husband through professional contacts. We were able become good friends within a short period of time as our thought processes matched in many ways. He invited me for a dinner at his home, and I realized that the couple looked very happy for the outer world, but did not seem that way in their hearts. I observed that they were not able to accept each other's views, and always try to choose different opinions.

I wanted to help this couple somehow. I invited my friend for lunch. I initiated the general topic towards personal relationships, apparently, he was not shown much interest to talk about it. Slowly, he started talking about his personal life as we were enjoying our meal. He said, his wife is really good at heart, but too childish at times, and he is not very happy with her behavior and stubborn nature. She is too much into friendships and keeps making phone calls to her friends and colleagues, at least ten times a day. He was not able to digest the fact that, there was no respect for his opinions and relationship when compare to her friends. He said, he requested her many times to change this behavior, but all his efforts were in the vein. It is quite obvious that, every husband and wife are possessive about each other in this world. She never cared about his opinion, and kept on doing whatever, she wanted to do. This type of behavior led to many arguments, and started widening the gap between them.

Relationship

I asked my friend not to worry too much about this situation such a simple matter. I told him, since they have no kids, his wife tries to engage with her friends just to kill the time. Then he mentioned, it is not about killing time, he strongly believes that, even if they had kids, she would behave the same way.

I gave my friend this advice to fix the problem…
I asked my friend to create a fake name, such as Ashley(a lady name) on his cell phone, and asked him to act as if he was talking to this lady in front of his wife for a couple of times. He started doing it for two times the same day. This kind of behavior increased the curiosity with his wife, and she tried to find out whom he was talking to. Soon she found the name Ashley on his cell phone, got irritated and warned him not to make any phone calls to Ashley again. He then replied, "I have been asking you same all these years." She started realizing how her husband would have been tortured with her stubborn behavior. She then decided to change her behavior immediately. She started paying more attention towards his husband and immediate family. They took a beautiful vacation, and fixed their problem permanently and living happily now.

I strongly believe in this formula - For every problem or situation you come across, put yourself in other person's position, and think through what would you do in that situation. I guarantee you that 90 percent of the problems you face today will just disappear, if you start thinking from other's perspective, and NOT for selfish reasons.

The bottom line: To achieve bliss in your life, you have to achieve success in your personal relationships first (if you're married). No human being born as a bad person on this earth; it is only the circumstances made the person grow up like that. Therefore, we have to start seeing the positive side of every person and accept and move on. Try to get married one more time or do the things which you like the most every year to rejuvenate your relationship. That way, it always remains as a year old relationship.

NETWORKING

Networking is a powerful tool for both personal and professional growth. The more contacts you have, the better it is for your growth. As we're in the social networking (web 3.0) era, networking becomes even more powerful and therefore, produces unbelievable results. True networking is engaging with people who have similar interests, and sharing ideas and thoughts. History proves that no creation is isolated. Groups of masterminds produce unbeatable results in comparison to that of an individual.

If you look at any business today, it is all about identifying and serving the customers with utmost care and keeping the customer base. In today's world, networking plays a critical role in identifying new business relationships and partnerships. No business lasts for more than a couple of months without any customers. Being an individual, you are no different from the business. You need to be associated with the right network for your personal growth.

I have attended many social networking gatherings, trade shows and business related events. I have observed that few people are effectively participating in these events. Most of them use these gatherings to sell their product or services without even passing the initial conversation. It is most unlikely that anybody would buy your services in the first meeting. Networking is about "connecting with the right people and establishing a relationship", and not about "I can sell right away." Nobody will show any interest if you go there and talk about yourself and your services and just throw them your business card. You need to establish a good rapport with people, identifying common interests, sharing ideas, and trying possible ways to make conversations more interesting. You can create miracles using the power of networking. Opportunities can come from any source, regardless of other's current job or position or status.

I would like to paraphrase another real situation here...

I have a habit of making connections with people, wherever I go. One day, I met this guy named Sean, who works in a hair salon. We were chatting about general things, and I happened to share with him my business and gave him my business card before I left. A week later, I got a call from the CEO of a logistics firm located in San Francisco, asking to learn more about our services. I was amazed with that call because Sean was just a worker at a hair salon. You never know where the lead generates from. Your job is to keep interacting with people and connect with them and to always be nice.

The bottom line: It is definitely not about the number of people you talk to. Quality is more important than quantity. Whenever you pay good attention in a conversation, you win their hearts instantly. More than the length of the conversation, the impression you left with the conversation is what matters. Connect first, and rest follows automatically.

LAW OF ATTRACTION

There is a lot of information floating around about the subject of "Law of Attraction". I tried my best to reveal "Law of Attraction" in a more effective, easiest, and practical way ever described before.

All human beings are a part of the universe (super source of all energies). The universe has created guidelines and laws to obey. Research says that there are thousands of thoughts flowing through the human mind every day, and some thoughts are significant and some are not. Every thought is carried by a significant amount of energy and vibration.

Good feelings generate positive vibrations and bad feeling generate negative vibrations. A human's subconscious mind transmits vibrations (positive/negative) to the universe and receives corresponding outcomes from the universe.

Just imagine how a mobile phone works. It simply sends and receives the signals based on your input. In simple words, if you call the right number, you get the right person. If you call the wrong number, you get the wrong person. It is all about what input you punch into the cell phone. Like the cell phone, the subconscious mind does not understand the difference between good input and bad input. It just acts as per your command.

The universe allows you to manifest anything you want upon impressing its guidelines and laws. At the same time, the universe also punishes you for violating the rules. Simply put, it's just like a law governed by a country.

General Universe Guidelines / Laws:

- ✓ The universe offers an abundant supply of wealth, health, happiness, success, you name it. There is no scarcity of a supply of these things whatsoever. Everybody has given equal share and right on this earth. It requires a lot of perseverance, patience, belief, and sincere effort to be successful. In simple words, everybody has born with a unique key to unlock their true potential in the universe. When you want something, it has already been delivered to your mailbox instantly. It is the matter of unlocking your mailbox and get it. Unfortunately, most of the people try to open the mailbox a couple of times and get tired and quit. A very few people are persistent with their acts and able to unlock the mailbox upon impressing the universe with their strong desire, dream, passion, persistence, commitment and by doing right things at the right timing in a right manner. The universe opens the doors for you to acquire whatever you want, only when you send positive signals attaching every detail of the thought. It is your job to make sure what kinds of vibrations you are sending to the universe. It is just impossible to open your door with the wrong key.

- ✓ The universe does not understand the difference between a positive vibration and a negative vibration. As mentioned

Law of Attraction

before, a mobile phone does not understand what your intentions are. It just follows your instructions. It is the same case with the universe. All positive thoughts which have been emotionalized and mixed with faith, begin immediately to translate themselves into their physical equivalent or counterpart.

✓ You have to show gratitude to the universe for whatever good you are enjoying today. It makes you feel good. When you feel good, you automatically send positive vibrations. For example;

  ❖ I have a great relationship. Thanks.
  ❖ I have a wonderful job. Thanks.
  ❖ I got promoted to higher position today. Thanks.

✓ The universe does not understand the general thoughts. It is most unlikely that you will manifest the general and ambiguous thoughts. For example;

  ❖ How nice it would be if I can make $200,000 per year.
  ❖ It will be a wonderful experience to drive BMW 7 series.
  ❖ I want to visit New Zealand at least one time in my life.

✓ In order to manifest any positive thoughts, you have to be very specific about every tiny detail. You should visualize the date, time, specific name, and every detail possible.

You should believe in your thoughts, and keep affirming the same thing at least a couple of times every day. Above all, you should be associate corresponding actions towards achieving these goals and follow every day. For example;

- ❖ I want to make $200,000 per year from 1st April 2010.
- ❖ I want to buy BMW 7 series (silver color) on 30th Sep 2010.
- ❖ I want to visit New Zealand between 10th-17th August 2010.

✓ Any negative thoughts or negative affirmations are bad signals and the universe produces the results as per your command or wish. Affirming words like "don't, not, no, never" are really bad for you. Indirectly, you're truly attracting those bad things more into your life. The more you think of those, the more you get those. You would never come out of the situation, unless you change your thought process. For example;

- ❖ I'm not lucky enough.
- ❖ I'm not happy with my job.
- ❖ My spouse would never allow me to be happy.
- ❖ I don't have a good relationship.
- ❖ I don't have enough money to pay my bills.
- ❖ The list goes on and on.

✓ If you are not happy with something, try to change the pattern or come out of the situation as quickly as possible rather than suffering with agony for a long time. If you do not, things will become even worse and go out of control. Letting go is the key to be free.

✓ There is nothing free in this world. It takes a sincere effort to achieve wealth, health, success and happiness. You have to be very practical before you wish for something. You cannot become a president of the United States without even understanding the basics of politics. Your desires should be aligned with your strengths and competencies and field of interest. You have the right to wish for BMW 7 series when you're sure to make $50,000 more this year. You have the right to wish for a six bedroom, brand new house in two years when you're confident about your skill set and future compensation. In fact, you can wish for anything you want, but you should know where to draw the line based on your strengths and limitations, considering the current circumstances.

✓ Act fast! Universe likes the people who act fast and over deliver than their promises. Remember, the reward for good work is more work. The better work you are assigned the more rewards comes to you. Most of the successful people are very quick in their decision making process and achieve desired results in no time.

✓ Master Mind - When a group of individual brains are coordinated and function in harmony, the increased energy created through that alliance, becomes available to every individual brain in the group. Find other people who are seeking the same definite purpose and meet with them regularly, or simply meet with a group of like-minded friends on a regular basis and take turns to brainstorm ideas for each person's definite major purpose. This practice would be very effective for creating a new venture or building a better organization.

✓ Affirmations - Positive affirmations are very essentials in life success. Universe always delivers whatever you want, if you can impress it with your strong beliefs, regular positive affirmations, and corrective actions. If want to climb up the big rock, the most challenging task is to get the wire hooked to the rock. And then, you pull the wire without much difficulty and reach the destination. Once you believe yourself that, you have already reached the destination even while you climb up, that belief will make the task much easier for you.

✓ Create a clear mental image/movie of your goal and watch it multiple times and believe that it has already been manifested and act as if you're enjoying it now. Universe manifests your wish much faster, when it receives the clear image and when you act as if you've already got it. For example, the historical movie Titanic may not have been produced, if James Cameron (Director) would not able to narrate scene-2-scene well to the producers though he created every scene in his own imagination. Producers would never want to invest in half-backed scripts. Universe is like a production company. Clarity matters!

Law of Attraction

✓ Ask the right question – Whenever you ask a sincere question yourself, your mind wanders through the universe and tries to find the right solution for you. I you need a car, believe yourself step ahead and ask, "how did I get this wonderful car as per my imagination?" – Universe answers your question by showing the way to find the car. This way, you are expediting the process by believing yourself even before it manifests. Remember, nothing happens without taking corrective actions.

Initially, you may have some doubt following these kinds of practices. Be practical and reasonable. Try to practice one thing at a time sincerely. You will understand the power of these universe laws. It works all the times. Universe always says that, "Your wish is my command". It is guaranteed!

I would like to share one real situation which I come across …

I was standing in the queue at Starbucks to get my breakfast. This guy Anthony was standing right next to me. He looked so tense and confused.

Venu: "Hello there! How are you?"

Anthony: "Hi! Good, you? I am rushing for an interview… Looks like a big queue here…"

Venu: "Oh! Good luck with your interview!"

Anthony: "(Giggles...) I know for sure I am not going to get through it."

Venu: "(A bit shocked) Why do you want to attend an interview when you know the result already?"

Anthony: "Well... Its my 11th interview in a row... I lost my confidence after the 3rd interview. I was doing my best but for one reason or another, I've been getting rejected continuously. These interviewers don't know what they're doing. What can I say?"

Venu: "Do not get me wrong... If you will allow me, I have a suggestion for you..."

Anthony: Sure

Venu: "Do not even bother to attend any interview until you are confident enough to face it. It is just waste of your time and energy. If I were you, I would strongly believe that I got the job already, and it is my first day at this office, as soon as I step in."

Anthony: "Oh, Yeah! You think so?"

Venu: "Of Course! You have to trust yourself. I would never waste my time doing something which I do not believe in. It is going to be a failure anyway. I have no time for failures."

Anthony: (Nodding his head...)

Law of Attraction

Venu:" Think about areas of improvement rather than blaming the interviewers. The moment you step into the office for attending an interview, you have to believe in yourself as if you got the job already, and it is your first day at work... "

Anthony: "Thank you! I learned something new today. Thanks for the coffee. You have a good day, sir."

Venu: "Good luck again!"

Interestingly, I happened to meet Anthony (dressed in a nice suite) at the same coffee shop after three months. He greeted me with a lot of affection and shook my hands firmly.

Venu: "How are doing?"

Anthony: "You know, Venu... I didn't attend that interview. I took a couple of days off and wrote on a piece of paper. What might have caused the failure of every interview which I attended? I realized a couple of things and promised myself not to repeat those again. I believed that I was going to win the next interview for sure. I had no other thoughts. I got the job three weeks after we met."

I shared the aforementioned universal laws with Anthony. I also asked him to share this simple process with his friends if believes in it.

- ❖ One goal at a time (something reasonable)
- ❖ Define specific time and date to achieve this goal

❖ Create a movie in your mind and watch it a couple of times everyday

❖ Take all the possible actions towards achieving the goal

❖ Believe as if you've already achieved it. You are in the process of finding the right key to open the box.

❖ Allow yourself to receive it

The bottom line: Manifestation is the process of translating the energy created (with your belief system) in your mind into the reality. Visualize not only the specific object/thing you want but the entire environment associated with it and all of its connections in the real world. Convert your dreams into images/ movies in your mind and keep watching them over repeatedly; Take corrective actions until you see them, in reality. If you follow the aforementioned sincerely, you will be amazed with the outcome.

SELF-MOTIVATION

If you want to achieve bigger goals in your life, you have to motivate yourself every single moment. Nothing can be achieved when there is no motivation. You have to divide every bigger goal into a group of multiple tasks and attach timelines and motivation factors to each one of them. You will be at your peak when you were complete one task and move on to another. It is also important to engage with people who have similar interests and motives.

Your job is to stay motivated at all times - read the biographies of top achievers in the field of interest; attend an inspirational seminars; conversation with top achievers; watch inspirational movies, etc. Belief is the basis of self-motivation - what the mind conceives and believes it will achieve. I told my niece (A 5th grade student) that, unless she gets a first rank in her class, it is considered as a fail. She believed in it and always strive hard to pass (get a first rank) in her class. It is your belief what leads to self-motivation.

The bottom line: Inspiration comes from outer world and motivation comes you're your inner world. Nothing moves without any self motives. If you're not motivated when wake up in the morning, you're wasting one productive day in your life.

SELF-CONFIDENCE

Self-confidence is an invaluable asset anybody could ever have. If the times are bad, you can lose your current position, wealth, health, happiness and anything you can possibly think of. However, you cannot lose your skills, wisdom, and self-confidence levels you have built over the years. Self-confidence is just enough to get everything back with even bigger bonuses.

Self-confidence gets built from awareness, knowledge, experience, and wisdom. The bigger the problems you solve, the more confidence you build. Self-reliance and self-confidence are correlated. You should not depend on others for any help too much. You should be able to make your own decisions by choosing the best possible solutions from mentors or through your own experiences. At the same time, you should be open to new ideas, thoughts and innovation to create a significant change in whatever you do.

The bottom line: Most of the successful people are self-reliant with great self-confidence levels. They believe in themselves more than anybody else in the world and always follow their heart.

BALANCE ENERGY LEVELS

The human brain is the storehouse of life energy. Life energy is used by the mind, the emotions, and the body, for it is involved in all processes of thought, feeling, emotion, and physical activity.

There are a lot of ways to generate raw energy for the human body: Regular exercises, walking, yoga, meditation, a good eight hour sleep at night, listening to good music, relaxation, diet, silence, positive thinking, setting up motivational goals, finding your purpose, learning new things every day, eating organic foods (fresh fruits, vegetables, nuts and seeds), dietary supplements, and fresh breeze, etc.

The brain consumes about 20 percent of the body's energy when at rest. So for a typical person, on an average day, this equates roughly to twenty-four watts (based on 2,400 calories a day). However, the energy usage of the brain does vary depending on the level of mental exertion. Studies have shown that when performing difficult mental activities, the energy usage of the brain increases. If you are performing greater mental activities, you tend to eat more without your knowledge.

Formula:

Based on a 2400 calorie diet on a day
2400 "food calories" = 2400 kcal

2400 kcal / 24 hr = 100 kcal/hr = 27.8 cal/sec = 116.38 J/s = 116 W

20% x 116 W = 23.3 W

Here are some examples of energy drainers: Skipping meals, stress, overeating, dissatisfaction with your job and personal relationships, dealing with negative people, too many electromagnetic radiations (watching too much TV, working on the computer for too long, and standing next to microwave etc), and polluted air.

Have you ever felt tired out of nowhere, and wondered why? These sudden energy slumps may very well result in the form of emotions such as:

❖ Grief
❖ Fear
❖ Jealousy
❖ Depression
❖ Anger
❖ Guilt
❖ Hostility
❖ Loneliness
❖ Resentment
❖ Sadness

The bottom line: You have to manage your diet and energy levels very well to be more productive and effective in your day to day activities. Use all your raw energy towards achieving your goals. Never allow yourself to spend any energy on unproductive things.

LEARN MORE ABOUT YOU

Unfortunately, a very few people spend time on learning more about themselves. For over a decade, I have been asking many people a simple question - "What do you know about yourself?". Surprisingly, I hardly got any spontaneous answer to this question. Most of them replied, "It's a good question. Let me think about that."

Just ask yourself –

Who am I?

What is the purpose of my life?

Where did I start?

Where am I now?

What is the motivation for my life?

Am I happy with my job now?

Am I happy with my relationship?

Where am I heading towards?

What is my core strength?

What is that I love to do?

What do I want to achieve in my life?

What drives me the most?

What makes me even happier?

If you have true answers for at least half of the aforementioned questions, then you are sailing towards your destiny. First of all, learning more about yourself gives you an edge and makes you transform from your current positions to where you want to be soon. Most of the successful people do have a clear idea about what their strengths are, and they pursue their dreams only in the lines of their interest.

You sit in an absolutely calm place or on the beach and start answering the aforementioned questions honestly to your heart. If you do not find an immediate answer for any question, try to dig more into yourself until you find the right answer. Once you have all the answers, try to map those with your current strengths and see the gap. You start working on the things which you lack, or on weaknesses by learning new things. Now you know about yourself well, so hook the thread to your destination and start pulling the thread until you reach the destination. You will reach your destination safely.

Learn More About You

Keep practicing the same exercise at least once a month. You will start to see a tremendous progress in your professional life, as well as in personal matters.

The bottom line: Try to learn more about who you truly are from your inner world not from the influences of outer world.

DO WHAT YOU LOVE

If you want to make a significant difference in the world, the single most important thing you can do is deliberately choose to work with what you are passionate about. No other choice can take you to greater heights on this planet. If you're doing work without passion, you never add any value to your life. If your goal is to not get fired from your current job, you will be stuck with the same job forever chanting the mantra so called "job security". No employer offers you security for your job forever; it is just your mindset. You are the only person who can safeguard your life.

If you are not passionate about what you do now, it is neither good for you nor your employer. Above all, it will drain all your energy levels, if you realize later point of time, you will regret for what you did all these years. Whatever job you do, it should be win-win for both the parties. Try to do what you love to do for a short period of time, and evaluate your performance, energy, and happiness levels. Indeed, you will understand the true power of doing the things which you passionate about.

Close your eyes (assuming you're given tons of time and money), just ask yourself a simple question, "What is that I love to do the most?" Now is the time!

One Book for Life Success

On June 12th 2005, Steve Jobs (Founder of Apple Computers) gave the wonderful commencement address at Stanford University in Palo Alto, California. As you may know, Apple Computers created the most innovative products in the century like iPod, iPhone, and most stylish computers and laptops, etc. Here is the transcript in his own words...

I am honored to be with you today at your commencement from one of the finest universities in the world. I never graduated from college. Truth be told, this is the closest I've ever gotten to a college graduation. Today I want to tell you three stories from my life. That's it. No big deal. Just three stories.

The first story is about connecting the dots

I dropped out of Reed College after the first 6 months, but then stayed around as a drop-in for another 18 months or so before I really quit. So why did I drop out?

It started before I was born. My biological mother was a young, unwed college graduate student, and she decided to put me up for adoption. She felt very strongly that I should be adopted by college graduates, so everything was all set for me to be adopted at birth by a lawyer and his wife. Except that when I popped out they decided at the last minute that they really wanted a girl. So my parents, who were on a waiting list, got a call in the middle of the night asking: "We have an unexpected baby boy; do you want him?" They said: "Of course." My biological mother later found out that my mother had never graduated from college and that my

Do What You Love

father had never graduated from high school. She refused to sign the final adoption papers. She only relented a few months later when my parents promised that I would someday go to college.

And 17 years later I did go to college. But I naively chose a college that was almost as expensive as Stanford, and all of my working-class parents' savings were being spent on my college tuition. After six months, I couldn't see the value in it. I had no idea what I wanted to do with my life and no idea how college was going to help me figure it out. And here I was spending all of the money my parents had saved their entire life. So I decided to drop out and trust that it would all work out OK. It was pretty scary at the time, but looking back it was one of the best decisions I ever made. The minute I dropped out I could stop taking the required classes that didn't interest me, and begin dropping in on the ones that looked interesting.

It wasn't all romantic. I didn't have a dorm room, so I slept on the floor in friends' rooms, I returned coke bottles for the 5¢ deposits to buy food with, and I would walk the 7 miles across town every Sunday night to get one good meal a week at the Hare Krishna temple. I loved it. And much of what I stumbled into by following my curiosity and intuition turned out to be priceless later on. Let me give you one example:

Reed College at that time offered perhaps the best calligraphy instruction in the country. Throughout the campus every poster, every label on every drawer, was beautifully hand calligraphed. Because I had dropped out and didn't have to take the normal classes, I decided to take a calligraphy class to learn how to do this. I learned about serif and san serif typefaces, about varying the amount of space between different letter combinations, about what makes great typography great. It was beautiful, historical, artistically subtle in a way that science can't capture, and I found it fascinating.

None of this had even a hope of any practical application in my life. But ten years later, when we were designing the first Macintosh computer, it all came back to me. And we designed it all into the Mac. It was the first computer with beautiful typography. If I had never dropped in on that single course in college, the Mac would have never had multiple typefaces or proportionally spaced fonts. And since Windows just copied the Mac, its likely that no personal computer would have them. If I had never dropped out, I would have never dropped in on this calligraphy class, and personal computers might not have the wonderful typography that they do. Of course it was impossible to connect the dots looking forward when I was in college. But it was very, very clear looking backwards ten years later.

Again, you can't connect the dots looking forward; you can only connect them looking backwards. So you have to trust that the dots will somehow connect in your future. You have to trust in something — your gut, destiny, life, karma, whatever. This approach has never let me down, and it has made all the difference in my life.

Do What You Love

Second story is about love and loss

I was lucky — I found what I loved to do early in life. Woz and I started Apple in my parents garage when I was 20. We worked hard, and in 10 years Apple had grown from just the two of us in a garage into a $2 billion company with over 4000 employees. We had just released our finest creation — the Macintosh — a year earlier, and I had just turned 30. And then I got fired. How can you get fired from a company you started? Well, as Apple grew we hired someone who I thought was very talented to run the company with me, and for the first year or so things went well. But then our visions of the future began to diverge and eventually we had a falling out. When we did, our Board of Directors sided with him. So at 30 I was out. And very publicly out. What had been the focus of my entire adult life was gone, and it was devastating.

I really didn't know what to do for a few months. I felt that I had let the previous generation of entrepreneurs down - that I had dropped the baton as it was being passed to me. I met with David Packard and Bob Noyce and tried to apologize for screwing up so badly. I was a very public failure, and I even thought about running away from the valley. But something slowly began to dawn on me — I still loved what I did. The turn of events at Apple had not changed that one bit. I had been rejected, but I was still in love. And so I decided to start over.

I didn't see it then, but it turned out that getting fired from Apple was the best thing that could have ever happened to me. The heaviness of being successful was replaced by the lightness of being a beginner again, less sure about everything. It freed me to enter one of the most creative periods of my life.

During the next five years, I started a company named NeXT, another company named Pixar, and fell in love with an amazing woman who would become my wife. Pixar went on to create the worlds first computer animated feature film, Toy Story, and is now the most successful animation studio in the world. In a remarkable turn of events, Apple bought NeXT, I returned to Apple, and the technology we developed at NeXT is at the heart of Apple's current renaissance. And Laurene and I have a wonderful family together.

I'm pretty sure none of this would have happened if I hadn't been fired from Apple. It was awful tasting medicine, but I guess the patient needed it. Sometimes life hits you in the head with a brick. Don't lose faith. I'm convinced that the only thing that kept me going was that I loved what I did. You've got to find what you love. And that is as true for your work as it is for your lovers. Your work is going to fill a large part of your life, and the only way to be truly satisfied is to do what you believe is great work. And the only way to do great work is to love what you do. If you haven't found it yet, keep looking. Don't settle. As with all matters of the heart, you'll know when you find it. And, like any great relationship, it just gets better and better as the years roll on. So keep looking until you find it. Don't settle.

Do What You Love

Third story is about death

When I was 17, I read a quote that went something like: "If you live each day as if it was your last, someday you'll most certainly be right." It made an impression on me, and since then, for the past 33 years, I have looked in the mirror every morning and asked myself: "If today were the last day of my life, would I want to do what I am about to do today?" And whenever the answer has been "No" for too many days in a row, I know I need to change something.

Remembering that I'll be dead soon is the most important tool I've ever encountered to help me make the big choices in life. Because almost everything — all external expectations, all pride, all fear of embarrassment or failure - these things just fall away in the face of death, leaving only what is truly important. Remembering that you are going to die is the best way I know to avoid the trap of thinking you have something to lose. You are already naked. There is no reason not to follow your heart.

About a year ago I was diagnosed with cancer. I had a scan at 7:30 in the morning, and it clearly showed a tumor on my pancreas. I didn't even know what a pancreas was. The doctors told me this was almost certainly a type of cancer that is incurable, and that I should expect to live no longer than three to six months. My doctor advised me to go home and get my affairs in order, which is doctor's code for prepare to die. It means to try to tell your kids everything you thought you'd have the next 10 years to tell them in just a few months. It means to make sure everything is buttoned up so that it will be as easy as possible for your family. It means to say your goodbyes.

I lived with that diagnosis all day. Later that evening I had a biopsy, where they stuck an endoscope down my throat, through my stomach and into my intestines, put a needle into my pancreas and got a few cells from the tumor. I was sedated, but my wife, who was there, told me that when they viewed the cells under a microscope the doctors started crying because it turned out to be a very rare form of pancreatic cancer that is curable with surgery. I had the surgery and I'm fine now.

This was the closest I've been to facing death, and I hope its the closest I get for a few more decades. Having lived through it, I can now say this to you with a bit more certainty than when death was a useful but purely intellectual concept:

No one wants to die. Even people who want to go to heaven don't want to die to get there. And yet death is the destination we all share. No one has ever escaped it. And that is as it should be, because Death is very likely the single best invention of Life. It is Life's change agent. It clears out the old to make way for the new. Right now the new is you, but someday not too long from now, you will gradually become the old and be cleared away. Sorry to be so dramatic, but it is quite true.

Your time is limited, so don't waste it living someone else's life. Don't be trapped by dogma — which is living with the results of other people's thinking. Don't let the noise of others' opinions drown out your own inner voice. And most important, have the courage to follow your heart and intuition. They somehow already know what you truly want to become. Everything else is secondary.

Do What You Love

When I was young, there was an amazing publication called The Whole Earth Catalog, which was one of the bibles of my generation. It was created by a fellow named Stewart Brand not far from here in Menlo Park, and he brought it to life with his poetic touch. This was in the late 1960's, before personal computers and desktop publishing, so it was all made with typewriters, scissors, and polaroid cameras. It was sort of like Google in paperback form, 35 years before Google came along: it was idealistic, and overflowing with neat tools and great notions.

Stewart and his team put out several issues of The Whole Earth Catalog, and then when it had run its course, they put out a final issue. It was the mid-1970s, and I was your age. On the back cover of their final issue was a photograph of an early morning country road, the kind you might find yourself hitchhiking on if you were so adventurous. Beneath it were the words: "Stay Hungry. Stay Foolish." It was their farewell message as they signed off. Stay Hungry. Stay Foolish. And I have always wished that for myself. And now, as you graduate to begin anew, I wish that for you.

Stay Hungry. Stay Foolish.

Thank you all very much.

The bottom line: There is no person achieved any success at peak against his passion in the history. If you do what you love, you can use maximum potential of your abilities and celebrate every moment.

LOOK FOR AN OPPORTUNITY IN EVERY SITUATION

Whatever the actions are under your control, the only person responsible for the consequences is YOU. There are lots of things that are not under your control. It is just not enough if you are a good driver on the road, the person who drives next to you should be good too. Every action which is not under your control happens for a reason. You have to consider every action whichever is not under your control, as an opportunity to groom yourself and believe that it was the best possible thing ever to happen to you. Sometimes, it will make you realize the importance of the action immediately; sometimes it takes a while to understand why it happened. It has always been that way.

I would like to paraphrase a real situation which I came across:

Peter does not have a college degree, and he is working two jobs (sixteen hours) non-stop everyday for over seven years. All the money he was making was not enough to make a decent living. However, he had a lot of good ideas which he did not have any time to materialize. Peter was like a machine, without much progress in his career and personal life. One bad morning, Peter got in a terrible accident on the freeway while on his way to work. One of his legs was severely damaged, and he got taken to the hospital. He had undergone major surgery on his leg and doctors told him that he couldn't run ever again, for the rest of his life. It was four weeks after this accident that I happened to go to the same hospital because one of my friends was blessed with a baby boy. Peter was in a wheel chair, being pushed by a nurse in the same lobby. I had sensed a terrible feeling by the look on his face, as if he had lost everything in his life. I asked him what happened.

Venu: "Peter, I am so sorry for you. However, you are still breathing, and that is what matters. Do not worry about the rest."

Peter: (Turned to me with an irritated look on his face...) "I lost both of my jobs and one of my legs. You think I should not be worried about this?

Venu: "I completely agree with you. Do not get me wrong. However, you should not be in the same mood for the rest of our life thinking about this incident. You have been working so hard for a long time. God wants to put you at rest for some time. Trust that it was the best possible things ever happened to you. You should break the current pattern and get into a good phase. It is a cycle." By the way, were you happy with your jobs?

Peter: "Hell, No... but they paid my bills and fed my mouth."

Venu: "Why is it that anybody would worry about losing a job which they hate so much? Consider this as an opportunity to rest on your body and soul for a couple of weeks and start looking for new opportunities when you are better."

Look for an Opportunity in Every Situation

Peter: "Are you kidding? How can I find a new job now? Can you help me?"

Venu: "You do not believe in your strengths. You have a decent professional background. If you are not able to secure a job, who else would get it? Start thinking loud. It is the right time for you to think about what you want to be and to create a new plan for your life (I gave him my card and left).

Peter: "Sounds Good... Let me think about it."

Peter wrote an email to me four months later with great news. He secured a job as a store manager at the dollar store. He challenged me on the same email that he would own at least a similar kind of store in the next two years. To my surprise, Peter could buy a struggling dollar store with the help of bank loans and friends within 18 months. He currently owns about 5 retail stores and three liquor stores, all within the span of five years. He recently called me and said "I only broke my leg but not my life. I now believe that, the accident was the best thing ever happened to me in my entire life. I am very grateful for your advice at the right time".

The bottom line: Everything happens for a reason. Always look at the positive side of every situation and take advantage of it for your growth.

BALANCE BETWEEN PROFESSIONAL AND PERSONAL LIVES

One thing that is very difficult about our day to day lives - BALANCE. It is very hard to balance our personal and professional lives, especially during working days. Most of the people cannot detach themselves from their work and they continue to be in the same mood for another eight hours after work. The very reason being, most of them do not know how to manage their time well. They think as if they're doing the greatest job in the world and forget to take care of their personal matters. That's when the crisis begins.

If you're truly a workaholic, that becomes your greatest strength as well as your greatest weakness. Any word suffixes with 'holic' is no good for you. During work hours, detach yourself completely from your family, friends, and social gathering activities and just focus on work unless if there is any emergency. If you can organize your work schedule and make each moment productive at the workplace, you will have plenty of time for your family or other personal things. Sometimes, you will be very busy traveling and may not have much time for the family, but you have to compensate the gap with a vacation or outing immediately after return.

We all work for a better living, but we should not live for the work.

Hard work is a very important factor to step up the ladder in our professional lives. However, it is necessary to make room for other activities to keep you energized every day. For example; fun with the family members; physical exercises, social gatherings, yoga, meditation, walking, listening to nice music, and so on. The more room you create for your personal activities, the more room you can create for your creativity. Otherwise, you become restless doing the same things over and over and act like a machine at workplace.

If you ask yourself an honest question about how balanced you are today, you will certainly have an answer right away. Excusing yourself from one of these things like, "Once I become rich, I will have a lot of time for the family or other personal things." There is no bad time for your personal activities; The kind of pleasure you get from personal life is a hundred times more than your professional life. At the same time, personal happiness would give you more mileage towards achieving even bigger goals.

The bottom line: The word "happiness" would lose its meaning to "sadness" when there is no balance between work and personal life. Do not wait for the right time; Life cannot be postponed. Now is the right time!

IDENTIFY THE ROLE MODEL AND TRY COMPETE

Whatever industry you work in or type of work you do, identify your role model to get yourself inspired every day. For instance, if you are in the investment field, consider Warren Buffet as your role model and learn everything about him, how he progressed in his life, make sure not to repeat the same mistakes he made and try to compete with him. If you are in the internet industry, think of Google's founders Larry Page and Sergey Brin and see if there is any way you can compete with them. There would be nothing worse than benchmarking your immediate environment- it limits your growth right there. Whenever you need any advice on your professional career or business, seek help from your role models or mentors directly or indirectly. If you can sit in a calm place and establish a connection with your role model through deep meditation, you will certainly get answers from them. You may find it hard to believe this formula, if you never tried this before. Just try once, it works all the times. Universe categorizes the people with similar interests and intellectual levels. Therefore, you will have a better reception connecting with the people you admire in your field of interest. It is guaranteed!

Every innovation creates new jobs and opportunities and makes the world a better place. Innovations are born only when you understand the problem areas and gaps in today's world. Think of the Guinness book of world records. There are always old records broken and new records created. Whoever top the list today, they only benchmarked with the previous records, and they tried their best to beat those records. You should think in the same way in the field of your interest.

Look at the world record progression of the mile run...

Accurate times for the mile run (1.609344 km) were not recorded until after 1850, when the first precisely measured running tracks were built. Foot racing had become popular in England by the 17th century, when footmen would race and their masters would wager on the result. By the 19th century "pedestrianism", as it was called, had become very popular.

The best times recorded in the 19th century were by professionals. Even after professional foot racing died out, it was not until 1915 that the professional record of 4:12¾ set by Walter George in 1886 was beaten by an amateur. Progression of the mile record accelerated in the 1930s, as newsreel coverage greatly popularized the sport, making stars out of milers such as Jules Ladoumègue, Jack Lovelock, and Glenn Cunningham. In the 1940s, Swedes Arne Andersson and Gunder Hägg lowered the record to just over four minutes (4:01.4) while racing was curtailed in the combatant countries due to World War II. After the war, it was John Landy of Australia and Britain's Roger Bannister who took up the challenge of being the first to break the fabled four minute mile barrier. Bannister did it first, and Landy did it 46 days later. By the end of the 20th century, the

122

Identify the Role Model and Try Compete

record had been lowered to 3:43.13, by Hicham El Guerrouj of Morocco in 1999.

The bottom line: Progression never ends. Always strive to be number one in the field of your interest. If you are the number one in the field of your interest, try to conquer yourself.

TIME MANAGEMENT

A recent study shows that 95% of the population works for employers. Most of the people simply trade the hours for the money in the corporate world. Eight-hour jobs will create an environment for survival but does not make you rich, unless you know how to play the odds. Of course, there is nothing wrong in working but the productivity is what matters. On average, we spend anywhere between 13-14 hours every working day for the work life. Here is how 13-14 hours a day plays out for a regular job: eight hours on the job; one hour for lunch; one to two hours for commute; one hour for gossip or discussing something about the work or the people at the workplace; one hour to start preparing for work; and one hour to rest after the work. Is this really productive?

For instance, if your hourly salary is $30/Hr for eight regular hours, it will be down to $18/Hr (approximated) with respect to thirteen to fourteen hours per day. If you believe in this simple calculation, you now know how much money you are losing every day.

Sometimes, we tend to put a lot of effort to achieve small results. No manager will care if you work for thirteen hours or fourteen hours directly or indirectly. All that matter is your real productivity. At the same time, if you're smart enough to accomplish the things faster, ask for more or spend that time in something more productive for yourself.

If you think deeply about yourself and where the real productivity is going towards, you will have the answer for sure. If you've created thoughts on the work you're involved in, prepare a plan and share with some of the executives you know in the company. Most of the executives look for innovation and accept the feedback from the employees. Because they know that there is an only thing that will keep the business running: Innovation. It also allows you to move up the ladder quickly.

Always strive hard to be productive in whatever the job you are involved in. If you are lucky enough and have the easiest job in the world, please be honest to yourself and tell your manager that you are ready for more tasks. By doing so, indirectly, you're creating an impression with your managers that you're honest and proactive. Remember that no job is permanent in any corporation, whether you are working for a fortune 500 company or a start-up. Your job is to perform to the peak every minute and prepare for the worst.

Look at the Pareto Principle, also known as 80-20 rule. More generally, the Pareto Principle is the observation (not law) that most things in life are not distributed evenly. It can mean all of the following things:

- ❖ 20% of the input creates 80% of the result
- ❖ 20% of the workers produce 80% of the result
- ❖ 20% of the customers create 80% of the revenue
- ❖ 20% of the bugs cause 80% of the crashes

Time Management

❖ 20% of the features cause 80% of the usage
And on and on…

20% of the workers could create 10% or 50% or 80% or 99% or even 100% of the result. Think about it — in a group of 100 workers, 20 could do all the work while the other 80 goof off. In that case, 20% of the workers did 100% of the work.

The bottom line: Work is all about making the business vision true by offering one's skill as best possible. Businesses are created to make money. Do not take advantage of work hours for any personal use, unless there are any family emergencies. Keep an eye on your clock closely and estimate your productivity. Do not waste your precious time discussing about useless things. We have a very small percent of population in the world, who manage their time very effectively, indeed, they're successful. TIME IS MORE VALUABLE THAN MONEY. Time only either appreciates or depreciates the value of money. In our world, time management is like your personal stock market.

OUT OF WORK?

Given the unprecedented economic situation, there were many people out of jobs throughout 2008 and 2009. The entire world was terrified with the economic situation and looking for a drastic change.

Despite the economic situation, we still see some new positions in some businesses if not in a big number of businesses like there used to be. There are some people who are able to find new jobs every day, but not as many people as before. If you think that it is not your fault but the economy, you're in a true illusion. You cannot blame anyone but yourself. It is truly your problem. If you're serious and persistent, then look for opportunities not only every day but every moment. You will be the winner despite the current situation. You no longer need to sit at home watching TV and gossiping about the job market and economy over the phone.

Let me paraphrase a real situation:

I love to spend my time at Starbucks if I find the time. I go there at least a couple of days in a week. I happened to find this guy Richard looking terrible, as if he had just lost everything in his life. Richard was looking at the classifieds in the newspaper and saying abusive words to him. He was sitting next to me, and I could hear him quite clearly. I felt like he needed some help. I could not stop myself from saying hello to this gentleman. I just said, "How is everything going?" His immediate answer was, "I am feeling terrible, man. This economy is getting worse every day" I asked Richard if I could take the liberty of giving him a piece of advice about securing a job. The good news was Richard was easy going and pretty open for any suggestions.

Venu: "When was the last time that you were in a good mood?"

Richard: "..it's been a while..."

Venu: "When did you lose your job?"

Richard: "Five months ago."

Venu: "How do you pay your bills now?"

Richard: "Some savings, unemployment insurance, and credit cards."

Venu: "How are you currently looking for a job?"

Richard: "Looking at the newspaper, jobs on websites, classifieds..."

Venu: "How many hours a day?"

Richard: "I used to spend four to five hours a day; Now two to three hours every day.."

Out of Work?

Venu: "What is your professional experience?"

Richard: "I have six years experience as a sales manager in a retail store."

If you observe the pattern of questions, I really did not care about Richard's professional experience until the end. It does not matter what kind of work you do, all that matter is what steps you have been following to fix the problem. I quickly figured out that Richard has been duplicating the time by following the same strategy for five months. If you follow some strategy for a week with no results, you have to change the strategy immediately and look for alternatives. If you keep following the same strategy, then one week becomes two weeks with no results; two weeks becomes four weeks with no results; one month becomes two months with no results; two months becomes four months with no results, and so on and so forth. It's that simple.

I advised Richard:

If you're working, you end up spending at least 13-14 hours on the job for commutation, lunch, and after the work hour gossips, etc. You have plenty of time now. There are plenty of jobs available in the market today. I do agree with you that the market is pretty bad. Despite the state of the current economy, if someone can secure a job today, why can't you be the one to get it? The person who got the job today is no different from you. However, that person understood the game plan: how to do things in a better way.

You need to keep asking yourself these questions: "What else can I do to help myself get a job?" or "What are all the options left now?"

Try to answer these questions every moment as sincerely as possible, and give it your complete attention. You can go anywhere you want, but you need to achieve at least some progress every day. Take a piece of paper and identify your actions for that day and work towards them. Make some phone calls to the people you know, use all of your professional references, and respond to job ads quickly. I told Richard firmly, " Do not allow anyone else's thoughts in your mind and stop talking to anyone who overrides your immediate goals". I started to notice Richard taking notes carefully. He said "Well, nice meeting you. I don't know you, but you made me think twice about productivity. Thanks again."

I happened to go to the same place two weeks later. I once again found Richard there. This time, he looked very professional, and seemed like he was in a hurry to get to work. Richard greeted me with a big smile and said "My dear friend, where have you been? I have been looking for you. I started looking for a job for sixteen hours a day, and guess what? I got the job a week after we met, and you deserve a lot of credit, I think." I felt very happy for Richard. When Richard invited me for lunch, I requested Richard help others if he comes across anyone looking for a job. Richard hugged me, and said, "Sure, I will." Sometimes good suggestions are worth millions when times are bad for people.

And another person I met was Amy in the business section of the Barnes & Noble book store.

Out of Work?

Amy seemed very professional at first. I was holding some interesting business books, and this attracted Amy. We started a little conversation. Amy was a senior consultant helping companies in terms of growth, strategy, etc. Indeed, Amy has a great educational background with a MBA from one of the top schools in the country, but she was a bit upset about not being able to find the right job for three months. Being in the consulting business myself, I had good contacts at that time. Interestingly, one of my clients was looking for a consultant, and it appeared that Amy would make a perfect fit. I then proposed to share the contact details with Amy. Amy immediately asked what would be the pay rate for that particular position. I disclosed the ballpark figures with her, but she felt it was too low for her credentials, and was not interested in pursuing any further. I respected Amy's decision, and we both left the book store. Given the slowdown of the economy in 2009, few employers are in a position to shell out fancy hourly rates to consultants. At the same time, once the employers see the value in having the right consultant, there are very few things stopping them from paying more.

Interestingly enough, I happened to meet Amy three weeks later in one of the conference events in San Francisco. Amy immediately asked me if the position which I discussed earlier was still open. Unfortunately, that position was already filled. Amy was a bit upset, and with a disappointed tone said, "Lately I realize that I lost a lot of opportunities with my stubborn attitude." I then told Amy, "You know, when the times are bad, you need to be flexible enough to accept the facts and take the job, even if it pays a bit lower than what you are used to."

When the times are testing you, it is always good to engage in some kind of job and then start looking for better opportunities. It is not difficult to find a job if anyone is serious enough and willing to work for sixteen hours just to secure a job. If Richard could do it, you can do it too.

If there is only one job available in the city where you live, there has to be one person who gets it. Ask yourself, "Why can't I be that person?"

The bottom line: You need to have a fire in the belly and put sincere effort during the tough times. Always try to differentiate from the crowd. Despite the economy and market conditions, every day somebody is hiring. There are lots of jobs out there unless you say to yourself there are NONE. If you do not find any job, try to create one for you and more for others.

FACE INTERVIEWS
WITH PASSION

Attending an interview is all about truly selling your skills and experiences. Therefore, you have to be a good sales person to sell your goods to the customer (which in this place, happens to be the employer) successfully. You do not have to worry, even if you are working for a small firm now and will be attending an interview for a Fortune 500 company. It is all about winning the hearts of a group of interviewers. Every time you attend an interview, act as if you are going to war and want to conquer interviewers with your interpersonal skills, knowledge, wisdom and the experience you have gained over the years. Go with an attitude - you will never want to get defeated.

Personal Pitch – Prepare a two to three minutes personal pitch to brief your education background, skills, strengths, passion, and experience. In fact, you can describe a lot of things in one minute if you prepare well.

Plan Ahead - Do your homework! Research the company and the position if possible, learn the background of the people you will meet at the interview. Try to impress them with your research about the company and their business.

Prepare for tough questions - Once you have finished with your research on the company and interviewers, start thinking to yourself, what would be the best possible question they might ask you during the interview. Prepare well to answer those questions. Always make it precise and elaborate more (If they are interested).

Dress well – Spending money on a nice suit would be the best investment if you are in the job market. Make sure the suit is well pressed, and it makes you look sharp. Never be casual, even if the company's standard attire at the business is casual. Always make a sincere attempt.

Smile – Nothing beats a smile when you meet with the interviewers or customers. Display possible "cool" manners.

Eye Contact – Always maintain eye contact with your interviewer.

Show confidence levels – Most of the employers buy from confidence. Show your confidence levels and express a "can-do" attitude (wherever appropriate).

Focus on value add – Though the employer would be interested in learning more about your previous experiences, mostly, they care about what kind of value you can bring to their organization. Try to map your answers with their corporate language, service offerings and value propositions. There is an old saying, "When in Rome, do as the Romans do."

Be Positive- In particular, avoid negative comments about the past employers.

Face Interviews with Passion

Never lose your temper – Some employers want to check your temper levels. They may try to ignite you with some irritating questions. Do not take anything personally. Maintain the same pace. All that matters is winning their hearts at the end of the discussion.

Pay the utmost attention – Listen! Listen! Listen actively. Never get distracted from the discussion.

Show enthusiasm – Employers would love to hire people who show a lot of interest towards their organization. Be prepared to convince them on why they have to hire you.

Encourage - Encourage the interviewer to share information about his or her company. Demonstrate your interest.

Create a mark - Before you deliver every sentence, process it, and make sure it's going to impress them.

If you follow the aforementioned sincerely, there is no reason why you have to fail any interview.

The bottom line: Attend interviews believing that you're already in. For some reason, if it does not work, try not to repeat the mistakes made and give yourself one more time.

WORKPLACE SKILLS

Over 95 percent of world population work as employees today. It is very important to understand the workplace skills to move up the ladder within a short span of time. Unfortunately, most people are very busy with their day to day jobs, and do not focus much on the organization and industry trends. Hence, they do not understand the big picture. Unless you understand the big picture, it will be impossible to move up the ladder. If you want to become a CEO of an organization in five years, start thinking like a CEO starting today. If you have a clear cut idea where you want to go, it will be easier for you to move up the steps in no time.

I would like to divide the workplace skills into different sections as below.

Interpersonal skills:

- ❖ Dress well
- ❖ Listen well
- ❖ Speak well
- ❖ Write well
- ❖ Read well
- ❖ Cultivate a smile
- ❖ Watch non-verbal expressions (body language) very carefully and deliver.

- ❖ Develop a perfect handshake
- ❖ Be punctual
- ❖ Be frank
- ❖ Establish a good personal rapport with the team

Professional Skills:

- ❖ Show Commitment
- ❖ Believe in teamwork
- ❖ Under promise and over deliver.
- ❖ Have fun in whatever you're doing.
- ❖ Develop unique style that gets you noticed.
- ❖ Be a problem solver
- ❖ Be proactive
- ❖ Open to learn new things
- ❖ Never be timid in the meetings; Always ask questions.
- ❖ Compliment people sincerely
- ❖ Do not gossip
- ❖ Stand up for others (If situation demands)
- ❖ Never lie.
- ❖ Accept the facts
- ❖ Do not curse
- ❖ Think BIG
- ❖ Focus on customer relationship management skills

Organizational Skills:

- ❖ Know about the vision and mission of the organization

Workplace Skills

- ❖ Know about the ethics and standard organization rules and employee rights well
- ❖ Know about the entire organization hierarchy
- ❖ Understand the industry competition and market capital figures
- ❖ Know the customer base and where the organization heading towards
- ❖ Know the background of your immediate supervisor
- ❖ Understand your immediate supervisor's style of management and responsibilities
- ❖ Know your job responsibilities and priorities very well
- ❖ Maintain healthy competition among the team members
- ❖ See every situation through your supervisor's eyes
- ❖ Develop unique style of executing the tasks
- ❖ Always act fast finishing the tasks.
- ❖ Help team members (if situation demands)
- ❖ Improve selling/sales skills
- ❖ Up-2-date with industry trends, organization growth rate, customer base, sales figures, marketing strategy, and current happenings etc
- ❖ Think out-of-box and try to add more value in terms of process improvements and customers etc; Recognition follows automatically; Let the promotions chase you;
- ❖ Be innovative and share new ideas/concepts with your senior management.
- ❖ Always look for an opportunity for your professional growth in the organization.
- ❖ Look for new opportunities outside if not many in the same organization

❖ Whenever there is a change of job, do not try to duplicate the same job as you did; Try to do at least 30% new things when compare to your previous job;

The bottom line: Always strive hard to move up the ladder at your workplace as quickly as possible.

MONEY

Money is a force. Money comes with an attraction. Money is the greatest attribute of riches. It is a concentrated symbol of energy and power in life. Like all forces in the universe, money obeys certain universal laws or principles as described in the 'Law of Attraction' section. By understanding those laws and acting appropriately, we gain a great power over money, enabling wealth and prosperity to come our way. Affirmations are usually very powerful in this respect - because material desires often come with stronger emotional attachments.

Think about what you most desire. It may not be hard cash, but what it can buy. Money has no meaning, if you do not know what you want to buy with it. Therefore, be very specific about material desires. Money follows.

If your desire is to have an abundance of money to fill your needs, practice this affirmation: "I always have an abundance of money to meet all my needs." Repeat it several times by visualizing and feeling how it is to already have the amount of money you desire. Feel as though it has already happened and that all your needs are more than satisfied. While in this state, hold yourself open to all the ways and means by which you will have money flow into your life to meet your every need.

Money management is equally important as money making. Investing money in right ways would multiply your money. Always look for good profits not small interest rate on the savings account.

The bottom Line: One of the famous quotes from Jim Rohn, "Money is usually attracted, not pursued"

LEADERSHIP

There are lots of definitions for the leadership. To true meaning of the leadership is – bring out the real leadership among the team members and help create leaders. Leaders were made, not born. There are millions of well-educated people around the world, who lack the knowledge of how to lead others. Unfortunately, a very few business schools are emphasizing on true leadership today. Most of the business schools focus on the management. There is a difference between the leadership and management. One of the famous quotes from Peter F. Drucker, "Management is doing things right; leadership is doing the right things." A true leader always focuses on grooming the team and unlocks the maximum potential of individuals.

Once a friend of mine, who was working as Technology Manager in one of the software development firms in the San Francisco Bay Area, mentioned that, he was not able to move up the ladder he feels like he was stuck. When I asked him, "how many of your direct reports, you moved up?". He was a bit irritated and said, "how does it linked with my growth?"…Then I said, "Your boss will never move you up, unless you move your team members up".

Assume that, there is a ladder with 20 steps to climb the tree to pluck the fruits. You are being the leader standing on the 15th step (5 more steps to go) and your team of 14 people standing from step1 to step14. You have to give more room to your team members and move the person standing on the step 14 to step15 so on so forth. It is the only way to reach step20. This way, you are moving everyone one step ahead including yourself. In simple words, never ever expect to get promoted without creating a replacement for your own job.

Leadership is a trust. I know a CEO of a technology company in Canada. He is very well-educated and highly motivated leader. His mission for life is to create 200 millionaires. Though his expectations were so high on the team, he made some wrong hires. He strived so hard to bring the best out of the team to create a unique business model. Due to lack of chemistry and heavy egos among the team, he lost his trust on the team. He then started acting like a manager and totally forgot about his mission. He started spending most of his time and energy working with the team on the day-2-day small activities and lost his momentum on what his job truly demands for. When I met with him recently, I quickly figured out the situation and offered him some stellar strategies to come out of the situation and stay focus on his mission.

A person will trust you only when you trust. Trust will be built from what you do; not what you say. Once you build the trust among the team, the team's productivity will increase 100+ times faster and everyone wins.

The bottom line: A group of people (Master mind) with similar interests, goals, vision and mission can create miracles in this world. It is only possible through the true leadership.

SUCCESS IS A JOURNEY

The great Earl Nightingale said, "Success is the progressive realization of a worthwhile goal." What he means is being successful is not just reaching your goal, but the continuous activity towards that goal. After all, there's no point in a person's life where they actually stop, look at what they have, and suddenly decide that's it, I have enough and I've made it to where I want to be. Do you think Bill Gates and Warren Buffet did that, or did they just set higher goals and aspirations and continue onward?

Success is a journey, not a final destination. You become successful as soon as you begin the journey. So if you're striving to reach a goal you are successful. If a new salesperson's initial goal is to sell 15 widgets a week, is his success concluded when he reaches that goal, of course not. They may have been successful, but the journey continues by setting new higher goals and objectives.

The successful people may have had more difficulties and challenges than other people, but they don't mention them. They reject the thought of failure at all times. Being successful is about striving to overcoming personal barriers and recognizing your own unique dreams. Success is the result of a combination of commitment, passion, and persistence on a never ending voyage. Make your entire life a part of one long successful journey.

The bottom Line: Your success depends on how well you can execute the opportunity presented to you. The secret of success lies in believing in yourself that you have been already successful, and you are in the process of conquering yourself to achieve even more.

UPS AND DOWNS

Life is a series of *UPs* and *DOWNs*. You have day and night, summer and winter. There is always an *UP* immediately after every *DOWN* and vice versa. No status is permanent, but it takes a lot of effort to maintain the same status when you are *UP*. It takes only a few seconds to fell down if you don't pay the same attention as you did while climbing *UP*.

There is no short route to up without passing through a *DOWN* phase. There is an old saying, "you do not enjoy the taste of sweet, unless you taste bitter". Every situation that makes you *DOWN* will create an opportunity for your life to improve. You will never mature without facing any challenges. The bigger the challenges you overcome, the stronger you become.

To be successful, you need to solve complex problems with passion and welcome more and more challenges into your life. Even if the situation drags you to a *DOWN* phase, you will not be worried much since you have already solved complex problems.

In fact, most successful people have their great moments in their *DOWN* phases. Successful people enjoy struggles in the process of achieving greater things. You can learn a lot of things in your *DOWN* phase. You can enjoy the luxuries on your *UP* phase but you have to maintain the same momentum to keep it going.

Donald Trump, Real Estate Empire lost billions in 90's...

When the real estate business collapsed in early nineties, Donald Trump was in an enormous debt. In fact, he owed almost $9 Billion to the banks and investors. Can you imagine a $9 Billion debt? It's almost impossible to even imagine that one person can ever achieve that amount of debt.

You would think that a 9 billion dollars debt might sound like the person in debt is in a desperate situation.

What did he do? Well, He didn't quit. He was very persistent and negotiated with the bankers. He was determined to pay everything back. He started working even harder, and to make a long story short: now Mr. Trump has gotten up from the hole and is doing better than ever.

Beating a 9 billion dollars debt requires a determinant mind. If at some point you feel like you've got a problem, you might as well remember Trump's example. Never give up and make your way. If somebody can manage to get rid of a 9 billion dollar debt, then certainly whatever the problem you face today, you can overcome too.

Harry Potter series of books and movies had become the biggest publishing success in the history of the books business and led to the creation of a multi-billion dollar business across the world. I would like to share about the author of Harry Potter, J K Rowling.

Ups and Downs

J K Rowling was born in Chipping Sodbury, Gloucestershire, England. She married a journalist in Portugal (he was Portuguese), and her daughter Jessica was born in 1993. Shortly after the birth of her daughter, the marriage ended in divorce and J K, along with her infant daughter, moved to Edinburgh, Scotland. These times were really challenging for her. It was during this time that she became determined to not only finish her Harry Potter 'wizard' novel, but to get it published. Often she would write in restaurants, where she and her daughter could stay warm while she wrote. She requested a grant from the Scottish Arts Council, which she eventually received, in order to complete her book. When it was completed and after several rejections, Ms. Rowling sold the novel, Harry Potter and The Philosopher's Stone, to Bloomsbury in the UK for the equivalent of about $4,000. Although her given name at birth was Joanne Kathleen, her publisher Bloomsbury feared that the target audience of young boys might be reluctant to buy books written by a female author, and requested that she use two initials, rather than reveal her first name.

Forbes has named J K Rowling as the first person to become a U.S.-dollar billionaire by writing books. It was wizardry that transformed J.K. Rowling from a destitute single mother on welfare into a best-selling billionaire. Her adventures of teenage magician Harry Potter and his classmates at Hogwarts became a children's literary sensation in 1998 with the U.S. publication of Harry Potter and the Sorcerer's Stone. It and the six subsequent books have now sold 375 million copies worldwide. Harry Potter and the Deathly Hallows, has sold over 44 million including 15 million in the first 24 hours.

One Book for Life Success

J K Rowling delivered an excellent commencement address, "The Fringe Benefits of Failure, and the Importance of Imagination," at the Annual Meeting of the Harvard Alumni Association in June 2008. Here is the text as delivered follows...

President Faust, members of the Harvard Corporation and the Board of Overseers, members of the faculty, proud parents, and, above all, graduates.

The first thing I would like to say is 'thank you.' Not only has Harvard given me an extraordinary honour, but the weeks of fear and nausea I have endured at the thought of giving this commencement address have made me lose weight. A win-win situation! Now all I have to do is take deep breaths, squint at the red banners and convince myself that I am at the world's largest Gryffindor reunion.

Delivering a commencement address is a great responsibility; or so I thought until I cast my mind back to my own graduation. The commencement speaker that day was the distinguished British philosopher Baroness Mary Warnock. Reflecting on her speech has helped me enormously in writing this one, because it turns out that I can't remember a single word she said. This liberating discovery enables me to proceed without any fear that I might inadvertently influence you to abandon promising careers in business, the law or politics for the giddy delights of becoming a gay wizard.

Ups and Downs

You see? If all you remember in years to come is the 'gay wizard' joke, I've come out ahead of Baroness Mary Warnock. Achievable goals: the first step to self improvement.

Actually, I have wracked my mind and heart for what I ought to say to you today. I have asked myself what I wish I had known at my own graduation, and what important lessons I have learned in the 21 years that have expired between that day and this.

I have come up with two answers. On this wonderful day when we are gathered together to celebrate your academic success, I have decided to talk to you about the benefits of failure. And as you stand on the threshold of what is sometimes called 'real life', I want to extol the crucial importance of imagination.

These may seem quixotic or paradoxical choices, but please bear with me.

Looking back at the 21-year-old that I was at graduation, is a slightly uncomfortable experience for the 42-year-old that she has become. Half my lifetime ago, I was striking an uneasy balance between the ambition I had for myself, and what those closest to me expected of me.

I was convinced that the only thing I wanted to do, ever, was to write novels. However, my parents, both of whom came from impoverished backgrounds and neither of whom had been to college, took the view that my overactive imagination was an amusing personal quirk that would never pay a mortgage, or secure a pension. I know that the irony strikes with the force of a cartoon anvil, now.

So they hoped that I would take a vocational degree; I wanted to study English Literature. A compromise was reached that in retrospect satisfied nobody, and I went up to study Modern Languages. Hardly had my parents' car rounded the corner at the end of the road than I ditched German and scuttled off down the Classics corridor.

I cannot remember telling my parents that I was studying Classics; they might well have found out for the first time on graduation day. Of all the subjects on this planet, I think they would have been hard put to name one less useful than Greek mythology when it came to securing the keys to an executive bathroom.

I would like to make it clear, in parenthesis, that I do not blame my parents for their point of view. There is an expiry date on blaming your parents for steering you in the wrong direction; the moment you are old enough to take the wheel, responsibility lies with you. What is more, I cannot criticize my parents for hoping that I would never experience poverty. They had been poor themselves, and I have since been poor, and I quite agree with them that it is not an ennobling experience. Poverty entails fear, and stress, and sometimes depression; it means a thousand petty humiliations and hardships. Climbing out of poverty by your own efforts, that is indeed something on which to pride yourself, but poverty itself is romanticized only by fools.

Ups and Downs

What I feared most for myself at your age was not poverty, but failure.

At your age, in spite of a distinct lack of motivation at university, where I had spent far too long in the coffee bar writing stories, and far too little time at lectures, I had a knack for passing examinations, and that, for years, had been the measure of success in my life and that of my peers.

I am not dull enough to suppose that because you are young, gifted and well-educated, you have never known hardship or heartbreak. Talent and intelligence never yet inoculated anyone against the caprice of the Fates, and I do not for a moment suppose that everyone here has enjoyed an existence of unruffled privilege and contentment.

However, the fact that you are graduating from Harvard suggests that you are not very well-acquainted with failure. You might be driven by a fear of failure quite as much as a desire for success. Indeed, your conception of failure might not be too far from the average person's idea of success, so high have you already flown.

Ultimately, we all have to decide for ourselves what constitutes failure, but the world is quite eager to give you a set of criteria if you let it. So I think it fair to say that by any conventional measure, a mere seven years after my graduation day, I had failed on an epic scale. An exceptionally short-lived marriage had imploded, and I was jobless, a lone parent, and as poor as it is possible to be in modern Britain, without being homeless. The fears that my parents had had for me, and that I had had for myself, had both come to pass, and by every usual standard, I was the biggest failure I knew.

Now, I am not going to stand here and tell you that failure is fun. That period of my life was a dark one, and I had no idea that there was going to be what the press has since represented as a kind of fairy tale resolution. I had no idea then how far the tunnel extended, and for a long time, any light at the end of it was a hope rather than a reality.

So why do I talk about the benefits of failure? Simply because failure meant a stripping away of the inessential. I stopped pretending to myself that I was anything other than what I was, and began to direct all my energy into finishing the only work that mattered to me. Had I really succeeded at anything else, I might never have found the determination to succeed in the one arena I believed I truly belonged. I was set free, because my greatest fear had been realized, and I was still alive, and I still had a daughter whom I adored, and I had an old typewriter and a big idea. And so rock bottom became the solid foundation on which I rebuilt my life.

You might never fail on the scale I did, but some failure in life is inevitable. It is impossible to live without failing at something, unless you live so cautiously that you might as well not have lived at all – in which case, you fail by default.

Failure gave me an inner security that I had never attained by passing examinations. Failure taught me things about myself that I could have learned no other way. I discovered that I had a strong will, and more discipline than I had suspected; I also found out that I had friends whose value was truly above the price of rubies.

The knowledge that you have emerged wiser and stronger from setbacks means that you are, ever after, secure in your ability to survive. You will never truly know yourself, or the strength of your relationships, until both have been tested by adversity. Such knowledge is a true gift, for all that it is painfully won, and it has been worth more than any qualification I ever earned.

So given a Time Turner, I would tell my 21-year-old self that personal happiness lies in knowing that life is not a check-list of acquisition or achievement. Your qualifications, your CV, are not your life, though you will meet many people of my age and older who confuse the two. Life is difficult, and complicated, and beyond anyone's total control, and the humility to know that will enable you to survive its vicissitudes.

Now you might think that I chose my second theme, the importance of imagination, because of the part it played in rebuilding my life, but that is not wholly so. Though I personally will defend the value of bedtime stories to my last gasp, I have learned to value imagination in a much broader sense. Imagination is not only the uniquely human capacity to envision that which is not, and therefore the fount of all invention and innovation. In its arguably most transformative and revelatory capacity, it is the power that enables us to empathize with humans whose experiences we have never shared.

One Book for Life Success

One of the greatest formative experiences of my life preceded Harry Potter, though it informed much of what I subsequently wrote in those books. This revelation came in the form of one of my earliest day jobs. Though I was sloping off to write stories during my lunch hours, I paid the rent in my early 20s by working at the African research department at Amnesty International's headquarters in London.

There in my little office I read hastily scribbled letters smuggled out of totalitarian regimes by men and women who were risking imprisonment to inform the outside world of what was happening to them. I saw photographs of those who had disappeared without trace, sent to Amnesty by their desperate families and friends. I read the testimony of torture victims and saw pictures of their injuries. I opened handwritten, eye-witness accounts of summary trials and executions, of kidnappings and rapes.

Many of my co-workers were ex-political prisoners, people who had been displaced from their homes, or fled into exile, because they had the temerity to speak against their governments. Visitors to our offices included those who had come to give information, or to try and find out what had happened to those they had left behind.

I shall never forget the African torture victim, a young man no older than I was at the time, who had become mentally ill after all he had endured in his homeland. He trembled uncontrollably as he spoke into a video camera about the brutality inflicted upon him. He was a foot taller than I was, and seemed as fragile as a child. I was given the job of escorting him back to the Underground Station afterwards, and this man whose life had been shattered by cruelty took my hand with exquisite courtesy, and wished me future happiness.

And as long as I live I shall remember walking along an empty corridor and suddenly hearing, from behind a closed door, a scream of pain and horror such as I have never heard since. The door opened, and the researcher poked out her head and told me to run and make a hot drink for the young man sitting with her. She had just had to give him the news that in retaliation for his own outspokenness against his country's regime, his mother had been seized and executed.

Every day of my working week in my early 20s I was reminded how incredibly fortunate I was, to live in a country with a democratically elected government, where legal representation and a public trial were the rights of everyone.

Every day, I saw more evidence about the evils humankind will inflict on their fellow humans, to gain or maintain power. I began to have nightmares, literal nightmares, about some of the things I saw, heard, and read.

And yet I also learned more about human goodness at Amnesty International than I had ever known before.

Amnesty mobilizes thousands of people who have never been tortured or imprisoned for their beliefs to act on behalf of those who have. The power of human empathy, leading to collective action, saves lives, and frees prisoners. Ordinary people, whose personal well-being and security are assured, join together in huge numbers to save people they do not know, and will never meet. My small participation in that process was one of the most humbling and inspiring experiences of my life.

Unlike any other creature on this planet, humans can learn and understand, without having experienced. They can think themselves into other people's places.

Of course, this is a power, like my brand of fictional magic, that is morally neutral. One might use such an ability to manipulate, or control, just as much as to understand or sympathize.

And many prefer not to exercise their imaginations at all. They choose to remain comfortably within the bounds of their own experience, never troubling to wonder how it would feel to have been born other than they are. They can refuse to hear screams or to peer inside cages; they can close their minds and hearts to any suffering that does not touch them personally; they can refuse to know.

I might be tempted to envy people who can live that way, except that I do not think they have any fewer nightmares than I do. Choosing to live in narrow spaces leads to a form of mental agoraphobia, and that brings its own terrors. I think the wilfully unimaginative see more monsters. They are often more afraid.

What is more, those who choose not to empathize enable real monsters. For without ever committing an act of outright evil ourselves, we collude with it, through our own apathy.

Ups and Downs

One of the many things I learned at the end of that Classics corridor down which I ventured at the age of 18, in search of something I could not then define, was this, written by the Greek author Plutarch: What we achieve inwardly will change outer reality.

That is an astonishing statement and yet proven a thousand times every day of our lives. It expresses, in part, our inescapable connection with the outside world, the fact that we touch other people's lives simply by existing.

But how much more are you, Harvard graduates of 2008, likely to touch other people's lives? Your intelligence, your capacity for hard work, the education you have earned and received, give you unique status, and unique responsibilities. Even your nationality sets you apart. The great majority of you belong to the world's only remaining superpower. The way you vote, the way you live, the way you protest, the pressure you bring to bear on your government, has an impact way beyond your borders. That is your privilege, and your burden.

If you choose to use your status and influence to raise your voice on behalf of those who have no voice; if you choose to identify not only with the powerful, but with the powerless; if you retain the ability to imagine yourself into the lives of those who do not have your advantages, then it will not only be your proud families who celebrate your existence, but thousands and millions of people whose reality you have helped change. We do not need magic to change the world, we carry all the power we need inside ourselves already: we have the power to imagine better.

I am nearly finished. I have one last hope for you, which is something that I already had at 21. The friends with whom I sat on graduation day have been my friends for life. They are my children's godparents, the people to whom I've been able to turn in times of trouble, people who have been kind enough not to sue me when I took their names for Death Eaters. At our graduation we were bound by enormous affection, by our shared experience of a time that could never come again, and, of course, by the knowledge that we held certain photographic evidence that would be exceptionally valuable if any of us ran for Prime Minister.

So today, I wish you nothing better than similar friendships. And tomorrow, I hope that even if you remember not a single word of mine, you remember those of Seneca, another of those old Romans I met when I fled down the Classics corridor, in retreat from career ladders, in search of ancient wisdom:

As is a tale, so is life: not how long it is, but how good it is, is what matters.

I wish you all very good lives.

Thank you very much.

The bottom line: Most of the successful people know the true difference between Ups and Downs. They do not worry, even if they lost everything what they acquired over the years. They use the same magic formula and get everything back, and even receive much bigger bonuses than before in a lesser amount of time. Do not expect to be successful in all your efforts the first time.

Ups and Downs

Consider failure as a small memory and success as the reality. Whatever you lost today should be considered as an investment towards achieving your next bigger goal. Sometimes you win, sometimes you learn, failure does not exist in the real world. Failure is an illusion.

MAJOR KEYS TO HAPPINESS AND SUCCESS

The One common thing that every human being is chasing in this world: Happiness. Assuming you have everything you want. You enjoy good health; you acquired millions; you are on an everlasting success path; you are famous – Even after all these, happiness is what matters the most. Wealth provides you security and safety; Good health makes you enjoy all the luxuries; Success increases your energy levels and network; Happiness demands you to do what you love the most in the world; Eventually, everything boils down to the happiness.

Discover your unique gifts
Every human being is born with unique gifts, because you have unique biometrics (Thump Impressions, Retina, IRIS etc). Most people do not know how to unlock their true potential. Therefore, they will be wandering around in life without any passion. If you ask yourself a sincere question about your unique strengths and interests, then you will have the answer.

Discover your passion
There are keys to your passion. One is your identity; who you are very different from what you do. Your profession might be a medical doctor but that doesn't mean you are in your true profession. Another key to your passion is your abilities. Skills and

abilities take years to be developed; unconsciously, each investment on your skill is also a matter of discovering your passion and purpose. If you close your eyes and think about what you want to do the most if given wealth, health, and success, then you will have the answer. Try to understand the purpose of your life. Otherwise, you are just setting yourself up for disappointment.

Develop a clear cut aim or goal
You have to have great clarity about your immediate goal including the material, date, time, quantity, measurement, and every minute detail.

Be a Magnet
We all know that every magnet has its own range and power. Smaller magnets draw smaller objects and larger magnets draw larger objects. The human magnet truly attracts the things based on their thoughts, beliefs, emotions, feelings, and imaginations.

Protect your health
Health is a key factor in your life. Without health, you can do nothing. Health is what makes you live rich. Exercise daily. Be moderate in eating and drinking. Chew your food thoroughly. Do not overeat emotionally. When you get to the point where you no more enjoy your food, you can stop it right there. Avoid emotional eating when you are not hungry.

Live in Future
There is an only direction to move in life – FORWARD. The past is dead and over. However, we can still benefit from the past; lessons learned; wisdom; experiences. You repeat the good things

and try to avoid the same mistakes. There is a personal punishment associated with every mistake you repeat. Most of the times, we tend to dwell in the past saying to ourselves things like, "It would have been better If I had that job."; "It would have been better if I had retained my house back without foreclosing"; "I would have achieved big success if my ex-wife had cooperated with me in my personal life"; The list goes on and on.

Remember, everything happens for a reason. You have to consider whatever happened to your life was the best possible thing ever to happen to you. There is no point in thinking about the past. You have to focus on NOW and the FUTURE and move on. Your job is to think always – What's next?

Preserve your energy for good

Never waste your energy in useless pursuits. Too much talking and gossiping, aimless wandering, habits of worrying, losing your temper frequently—all these drain your energy away. Give up all habits that are likely to have an adverse effect on your health. Smoking and illegal drugs are the worst. Develop physical and mental strength and thus lay the foundation of a successful life. Never lose your momentum. Stay away from negative thoughts and negative people. Use all your raw energy towards achieving your goals.

Build Character

Value character is the most precious thing on earth. Do not let your speech be vulgar or rude. Speech must be clean, polite, and joy-giving. Cast away the most dangerous traits like egoism, pride and selfishness. They arise out of ignorance and greed. Ignorance makes you proud and egotistic. Greed makes you selfish. They lead to dishonor and unhappiness and failure in life. By leading a simple life and having a cheerful disposition under all circumstances, you can overcome selfishness and egoism. Your life and conduct must be the cause of happiness in other people.

It takes every second to build the character but takes only one second to lose. If wealth is lost, nothing is lost; if health is lost, something is lost; if the character is lost, everything is lost.

Be Honest

Even at the cost of your life, never utter falsehood. It pays off big time in the long run. Never be dishonest in any of your dealings with anyone in the world. Become established in truthfulness in thought, word, and deed.

Just do what you love the most

You should take pride in what you love to do, even if it is scorned or misunderstood or criticized by the public at large. Ask yourself a simple question – "If time and money were not an issue what would I do with my life?" If you can answer this question honestly, you are on your success path already.

Help Others

Helping others bring good feelings to the giver and the receiver of the good deeds. Using your special gifts to help others can be a gift to yourself as you enjoy a self esteem boost for making others' lives better, and making the world a better place. You feel more worthy of good deeds yourself, your trust in the decency of people is reinforced, and you feel more connected to yourself and to others. In fact, research shows that those who demonstrate more altruistic social interest tend to enjoy higher levels of mental health, above and beyond the practical benefits of receiving help and other known stress, and demographic factors that you would expect. The more you give it to others, the more it comes to you.

Never Relax

The moment you start relaxing with your previous/current accomplishments, you are losing your momentum and putting yourself into a down phase. Always try to find new ways to improve your personal and professional skills and promise yourself to achieve even bigger goals than before.

Act Fast

If you believe in something, act upon it immediately. Otherwise, you will forget it after some time. Waiting is the waste of time. You have to act as if you were to die tomorrow.

Review your progress

You are no different from the business. Like a public company broadcasts its quarterly results (once in every 3 months) to the public in terms their performance, accomplishments, the gap between the target and the actual revenues, future plans, and promises - review your personal growth, accomplishment and promise your future achievements with your families, friends, colleagues, relatives, loved ones and more. It is a very powerful technique. In case, if you do not want to share with others well in advance, at least stand in front of the mirror and make a sincere promise to yourself. Once you commit, you have no other choice but exceed the expectations.

Results what matters not the actions
Always think in terms of the end result when you engage in any activity. At the end of the day, all that truly matters is the true outcome of a series of actions. In simple words, at any given moment, the outcome is what you can see in real not your past actions. No matter how many hurdles the farmer had to go through in the process of growing the crop, it is only the fruits which give him/her happiness.

Always take the feedback
Listen well to others' comments and take the feedback (if appropriate). Cultivate relationships with people and try to find good mentors and books in the area of your interest. Then weigh your own options and pick the best out of best – you are the decision maker anyway. If you do not care about others' opinion at all, there is good chance that, you may repeat the same mistakes what others' did. It is not wise to spend the same amount of time when you have access to the library of DOs and DONT's.

Handling Pressure
Nothing comes to you so easily. If there is any such easy thing, soon you realize the timeless fact, "Easy come and Easy go". Life tests you in many ways before it certifies you as a successful person. It is like doing PhD in the subject of success. Therefore, you must be prepared to undergo lots of pressures to achieve bigger goals. Your success rate is truly proportionate to how much pressure you can handle when the times are challenging.

Major Keys to Happiness and Success

Always Be Productive

Before you invest a single moment on any activity, just ask yourself a question "In what way this action would add value in my life". If you see no significant value, just come out of it without wasting a second. You would be amazed how much time most of the people waste for non-productive activities every day. If you can double your productity, you can double your success rate too.

Inspire yourself every moment

Do whatever it takes to inspire you at all times. Watch your mood every moment cautiously and never allow yourself for disappointment. If you're upset, for some reason, take an immediate action to change your mood – talk to loved ones, read a book, listen to a nice music, watch an inspirational movie, shop around, try to recollect the funny events which you come across, etc.

Never, Ever Quit

A quitter never wins, and winner never quits. Demand yourself one more punch until you reach your goal.

Watch your own movies every day

You need to create a movie with very specific goal and timeline and watch it almost every day. Self-affirmation is very important in life. You are the script writer, music composer, producer, director, actor, and critic. The more you watch the same movie, the faster you can manifest it into the reality. There is no cost associated with it, absolutely free. Award an Oscar within yourself for every movie you made into reality successfully.

Celebrate your life everyday

Life is very simple, you are meant to have fun every moment not to get distracted with negative things. You are the system. You create laws for yourself and obey them sincerely. Always have a smile on your face by looking at your bright future. Just celebrate your life every moment as it comes!

GREATEST FAILURES OF ICONS

If you never failed, you never succeeded. There are a great number of failures behind every successful person. I would like to share some of the famous failures of icons in the history. Each time you face any failure or disappointing event or undesirable outcome, never forget some of these famous failures:

Thomas Edison

Thomas Edison had a teacher who told him he was "too stupid to learn anything." His teacher suggested he go into a field where he might succeed based less on intelligence and more on his pleasant personality. When he set out on his own, he tried more than 9,000 experiments before he created the first successful light bulb. If Edison had quit after five attempts or even 500 attempts you might still be reading by gas or candlelight. Edison developed many devices which greatly influenced life in the 20th century. Edison is considered one of the most prolific inventors in history, holding 1,093 U.S patents to his name.

Walter Disney

Disney started his own business from his home garage and his very first cartoon production went bankrupt. Disney had once been fired by a news paper editor who told him "he had no good ideas in film production". Walter Disney was reportedly turned down by 321 banks before he got the funding he needed to build Disneyland.

Walter Disney was American film producer, director, screenwriter, voice actor, and animator. One of the most well-known motion picture producers in the world, Disney founded a production company, Walt Disney, one of the largest productions houses today.

Frederick W. Smith

He received a nearly failing grade for a business idea he presented to his business management class while studying at Yale University. He believed parcels could be delivered overnight at a profit using a private airline system with a centralized hub. Hence the idea of FedEx was born. Smith succeeded in raising the money to start his business, but on Federal Express's first night of operation, the business shipped only 186 packages. In the first three months, Federal Express lost more than $30 million, and drivers often had to pay for gas out of their own pockets. On the verge of declaring bankruptcy, Smith renegotiated his banks loans and kept his fledging business going. Rest is the history.

Soichiro Honda

Soichiro Honda was turned down by Toyota Motor Corporation during a job interview as "engineer". He continued to be jobless until his neighbors starting buying his "home-made scooters". Subsequently, he set out on his own to start his own company, Honda. Today, the company has grown to become the world's largest motorcycle manufacturer and one of the most profitable automakers.

Greatest Failures of Icons

Steven Spielberg

During his childhood, Spielberg dropped out of junior high school. He was persuaded to come back and was placed in a learning-disabled class. He only lasted a month and then dropped out of school. He was rejected three times from UCLA film school because of his poor grades. Steven Spielberg is an American film director. He has won 3 Academy Awards and ranks among the most successful filmmakers in the history. Most of all, Steven was recognized as the financially most successful motion picture director of all time.

Oprah Winfrey

Oprah Winfrey was not born with a silver spoon in her mouth. In fact, Oprah Winfrey childhood began in poverty in Mississippi. She began her television career as a news anchor in Baltimore, but she was fired because executives thought she did not project herself as a hard-nosed reporter. And she had a weight problem. Winfrey accepted an job took AM Chicago from the bottom of the ratings to the top. A year later, the show renamed as – The Oprah Winfrey Show – rest is the history. Today Winfrey's talk show is the highest-rated in television history.

Albert Einstein

Albert Einstein was 4 years old before he could speak. He did not read until he was seven, and his poor performance in elementary school caused many people suspect he was mentally retarded. When the teachers called on him, the boy was mouthing the words himself before slowly uttering them aloud. The teacher told him that he would not become anybody in life. The boy went on to

175

revolutionize modern physics when he proposed the Theory of Relativity. In 1921, he was awarded the Nobel Prize in Physics.

Alexander Graham Bell

When he invented a communication machine, in 1876, it did not ring off the hook with calls from potential backers. After making a demonstration call, President Rutherford Hayes said, "That's an amazing invention, but who would ever want to see one of them?". Today, we cannot imagine a world without telephone.

Dhirubhai Ambani

Dhirubhai Ambani(Indian rags-to-riches business tycoon) was born at Kukaswada near Chorwad, state of Gujarat, India. He chose works which uses his physical ability to the maximum rather than mugging up school lessons. When his mother once asked Dhirubhai and his brother to help his father by earning money, he angrily replied "Why do you keep screaming for money? I will make heaps of money one day". During weekends, he began setting up onion/potato fries stall at village fairs and made extra money which he gave to his mother. When he was 16 years old, he moved to Aden, Yemen. He worked with A. Besse & Co. for a salary of Rupees 300 (US$6). Dhirubhai Ambani eventually returned to India and started "Majin" in partnership with Champaklal Damani, his second cousin, who used to be with him in Aden, Yemen. Dhirubhai had started the business with just Rupees 15,000 (US$300). He courted controversy all throughout his life. A lot of his competitors was not able to digest his personal growth tried to stop him in every move he made. He overcame tons of challenges with his courageous nature in his life time. He took his company (Reliance) public in 1977. He once had a major stroke in February 1986 and had kept his right hand paralyzed. He died on July 6, 2002. By 2007, the combined fortune of the family (sons Mukesh Ambani and Anil Ambani) was over 60 billion dollars, making the Ambanis the richest family in the world.

LIFE SUCCESS QUOTES

Try to remember and apply some of these wonderful quotes in your day-2-day life wherever appropriate. There is a great philosophy and wisdom associated with every quote you read. Whenever you disappoint with any event or not happy, come back and read these quotes, I guarantee you that, you can find instant relief and get some insight from one of these quotes.

To be a successful, act like one who walks on it.
~Venu G. Somineni(Author)

Never stop listening to your heart until the last moment.
~Venu G. Somineni(Author)

Happiness does not come to you; but it comes from within you.
~Venu G. Somineni(Author)

The reason behind a very small percentage of the world population is successful, because a lot of them have no goals at all.
~Venu G. Somineni(Author)

There is nothing worse than living in the past.
~Venu G. Somineni(Author)

Hiding truth is like holding the air balloon under the water; it is hard to hold for a long time; it can float onto the water anytime.
~Venu G. Somineni(Author)

The most inexpensive yet powerful thing in the world is your innovative thought.
~Venu G. Somineni(Author)

I don't know you before I've born; I'm not going to remember you after I die; why fight in between;
~Venu G. Somineni(Author)

There are no shortcuts in life – Easy come, Easy go.
~Venu G. Somineni(Author)

A person can lose everything in his life but self-confidence.
~Venu G. Somineni(Author)

The moment may come on the courage of man fails but not this moment.
~Venu G. Somineni(Author)

Life Success Quotes

You never understand your true potential, unless you dig into yourself more and more.
~Venu G. Somineni(Author)

Once the true war starts within you to achieve big, you don't remember the reason for the war any more.
~Venu G. Somineni(Author)

It doesn't matter how beautiful the things around you; all it matters is how good your mood at this moment.
~Venu G. Somineni(Author)

If something has not been happening yet, you have not believed it enough.
~Venu G. Somineni(Author)

A genuine person is someone who claps for others' successes and extends help to others when the times are challenging.
~Venu G. Somineni(Author)

A successful person is someone who truly understands the distance between where he/she stands now and the destination of his/her life.
~Venu G. Somineni(Author)

The secret of happiness is – promise yourself to be happy always with no negative distractions.
~Venu G. Somineni(Author)

If you ever lost in the life somewhere, consider that there was a tsunami came into your life but you're still breathing. Let's rebuild it from scratch by taking all the best possible precautions in a lesser time than before.
~Venu G. Somineni(Author)

If you want something, be very specific and go get it now. Period! Confusion state always confuses with confusions.
~Venu G. Somineni(Author)

Your negative thoughts are not cared about you as much as you do.
~Venu G. Somineni(Author)

No one believes you, unless you believe yourself.
~Venu G. Somineni(Author)

In spite of how successful and wealthy person you are today, never get carried away with the current status but always remember who truly you are.
~Venu G. Somineni(Author)

Life Success Quotes

The secret of true success is believing in yourself that you have been already successful, and you are in the process of conquering yourself to achieve even more.
~Venu G. Somineni(Author)

A true leader is someone, who spends 40% of his time for today and rest for tomorrow.
~Venu G. Somineni(Author)

There is no better fortune teller other than you; There is no worst destructor other than you.
~Venu G. Somineni(Author)

I am yet to meet a successful person who does not have fire in the belly.
~Venu G. Somineni(Author)

Postponing your current actions is like postponing your future; Life cannot be postponed.
~Venu G. Somineni(Author)

Success comes to those who always think about it by knowing the secrets.
~Venu G. Somineni(Author)

Age does not count when the mileage overwrites it; It is not about the age but mileage;
~Venu G. Somineni(Author)

When you remember the importance of innovation, you will forget about the competition.
~Venu G. Somineni(Author)

Sometimes you win, sometimes you learn, failure does not exist in the real world; Failure is an illusion.
~Venu G. Somineni(Author)

The only way of finding the limits of the possible is by going beyond them into the impossible.
~Arthur C. Clarke

One day is worth two tomorrows.
~Benjamin Franklin

For every minute you are angry you lose sixty seconds of happiness.
~Ralph Waldo Emerson

The greatest mistake a man can ever make is to be afraid of making one.
~Elbert Hubbard

Life Success Quotes

To accomplish great things, we must not only act, but also dream, not only plan, but also believe.
~Anatole France

Formal education will make you a living; self-education will make you a fortune.
~Jim Rohn

The people who get on in this world are the people who get up and look for the circumstances they want and if they can't find them, make them.
~George Bernard Shaw

We make a living by what we get. We make a life by what we give.
~Winston Churchill

When one door closes another door opens; but we often look so long and so regretfully upon the closed door, that we do not see the ones which open for us.
~Alexander Graham Bell

The significant problems we have cannot be solved at the same level of thinking with which we created them.
~Albert Einstein

One Book for Life Success

Success means doing the best we can with what we have. Success is the doing, not the getting; in the trying, not the triumph. Success is a personal standard, reaching for the highest that is in us, becoming all that we can be.
~Zig Ziglar

Many of life's failure are people who did not realize how close they were to success when they gave up.
~Thomas A. Edison

Nothing can stop the man with the right mental attitude from achieving his goal; Nothing on earth can help the man with the wrong mental attitude.
~Thomas Jefferson

Concentration of effort and the habit of working with a definite chief aim two of the essential factors in success which are always found together; Once leads to the other.
~Napoleon Hill

Management is doing things right; leadership is doing the right things.
~Peter F. Drucker

Life Success Quotes

Our greatest glory is not in never falling, but in rising every time we fall.
~Confucius

The best and most beautiful things in the world cannot be seen, not touched..but are felt in the heart.
~Helen Keller

It is our choices that show what we truly are, far more than our abilities.
~J.K.Rowling

Good ideas are not adopted automatically. They must be driven into practice with courageous patience.
~Hyman Rickover

Ignorance and inconsideration are the two great causes of the ruin of mankind.
~John Tillotson

Whether you think you can or whether you think you can't, you're right.
~Henry Ford

THANK YOU NOTE FROM THE AUTHOR

I hope you enjoyed reading this book. As you know, knowledge and wisdom are the best gifts you would ever want to share with your families, friends, relatives, students, and loved ones. I wish this book would help to unleash your true potential. Try to map aforementioned practices, tips, wisdom, quotes into your day-2-day activities. Just try once before you give up, you will understand the true power of these secrets. If you like this book please spread the word around. I wish you lead your life the way you want and exceed your expectations.

New Books (coming up….)

❖ **One Book for Sales & Marketing** – Everything you want to know about Selling and Marketing; Customer Relationship Management; Stellar business development techniques and tools; lead generation techniques; Networking; How to attract, retain and marry customers for decades and more

❖ **One Book for an Aspiring Entrepreneur** – How an entrepreneur born; how to bring the maximum potential of an individual; what it takes to transcend the current position to the executive level; how to create a new venture; how to get funded; how to groom the stellar teams; Deals with leadership skills and many more

- ❖ **One Book for Business**– A 360 degree view, everything you want to know about the business – what is the purpose of business; accelerate innovation; organization growth strategies; leadership; change management; people management; how to hire, motivate, and retain the best talented; how to overcome corporate politics; how to develop stellar sales & marketing plans and attract customers every day; cost reduction strategies; how to compete in the global market and many more

To learn more or order copies of this book, please visit
www.onebookforlifesuccess.com;
www.outskirtspress.com/lifesuccess;
www.amazon.com;
www.bn.com;
YouTube Keywords: Venu Somineni; One book for Life Success;
Write a life question: venu@onebookforlifesuccess.com

- Venu G. Somineni, Author

REFERENCES

http://www.forbes.com/2009/04/02/billionaire-clusters-harvard-skull-and-bones-goldman-business-billionaires-wealth.html

http://hypertextbook.com/facts/2001/JacquelineLing.shtml

http://www.cybernation.com/lincoln/persistence.php

http://en.wikiquote.org/wiki/Mother_Teresa

http://www.rogerknapp.com/inspire/lincoln.htm

http://stress.about.com/od/positiveattitude/qt/helping.htm

http://money.cnn.com/2006/06/25/magazines/fortune/charity1.fortune/

http://www.inc.com/magazine/20070601/hidi-wang.html

http://quotations.about.com

http://thinkexist.com/quotations/

http://www.selfgrowth.com/quote.html

http://www.census.gov/main/www/popclock.html

http://lessonsinlifemastery.blogspot.com/

http://www.google.com/finance?q=NYSE:WMT

http://www.brainyquote.com/quotes/topics/topic_success.html

http://www.wikipedia.org/

http://news-service.stanford.edu/news/2005/june15/jobs-061505.html

http://www.forbes.com/lists/2008/53/celebrities08_JK-Rowling_CRTT.html

http://harvardmagazine.com/commencement/the-fringe-benefits-failure-the-importance-imagination

http://www.famous-quotes-and-quotations.com

Book – Think and Grow Rich by Napoleon Hill

Book - Trump 101: The Way to Success by Donald Trump

Book - Sam Walton: Made in America by Sam Walton

LaVergne, TN USA
18 December 2009
167338LV00003B/3/P